MARRIAGE
ON THE
ROCKS

Learning to Live with Yourself and an Alcoholic

Janet Geringer Woititz, Ed.D.

D0036732

Health Communications, Inc.
Deerfield Beach, Florida

www.hcibooks.com

Excerpts from BORN TO WIN: TRANSACTIONAL ANALYSIS WITH GESTALT EXPERIMENTS by Muriel James and Dorothy Jongeward: Copyright ©1971, by permission of Addison-Wesley Publishing Co., Reading, Mass.

Excerpts from KNOTS by R.D. Laing: Copyright ©1970 by The R.D. Laing Trust. Reprinted by permission of Pantheon Books, a Division of Random House, Inc.

Library of Congress Cataloging-in-Publication Data is available through the Library of Congress.

© 1979 Janet G. Woititz
ISBN-13: 978-0-932194-17-6
ISBN-10: 0-932194-17-6
ISBN-13: 978-0-7573-1640-1 (ebook)
ISBN-10: 0-7573-1640-9 (ebook)

Publisher: Health Communications, Inc.
            3201 S.W. 15th Street
            Deerfield Beach, FL 33442-8190
R-9-11

Cover redesign by Lawna Patterson Oldfield
Inside book redesign by Dawn Grove

This book is dedicated to
those of you who live with alcoholic
husbands in the hope that it will lead you
out of the maze of hopelessness and
despair into a full, rich and happy life,
whether or not your husband
stops drinking.

CONTENTS

ACKNOWLEDGMENTS

I want to thank my children—David, Lisa and Daniel—for encouraging me in my work and for adding a special quality to my life.

Jan

INTRODUCTION

The National Council on Alcoholism estimates that there are 10 million alcoholics in this country. Each one of these profoundly affects the lives of at least six other people. The figures are staggering, and, I suspect, conservative.

Much attention has been given in recent years to understanding alcoholism and working with alcoholics. This work is vitally important. Unfortunately, not enough attention has been given to the family. The theory has been that if the alcoholic recovers, the family will recover. This theory is somewhat simplistic for several reasons. First, it dooms the family that's alcoholic does not recover. Second, it assumes that the family recovery can start only after the alcoholic's recovery starts, and third, it does not take into account that the family can be as sick as, if not sicker than, the alcoholic.

A family that comes to grips with the problem can play an important part in the recovery of the alcoholic, but the family's own recovery is important enough to treat separately. That is what this book is about—how families of alcoholics can help themselves to recover.

What I have discussed in this book, for the most part, is the stereotypic American nuclear family. The husband is the primary breadwinner and the wife is the homemaker who takes care of their 2.3 children. Although this is only one domestic style, it is probably the one that is still considered the most common. The discussion of one model also helps to keep the ideas somewhat simple. As you will see, the dynamics operating within the alcoholic family system get very complicated very quickly.

There are many other models that can be developed to look at alcoholism within a family. There is the situation where the wife and not the husband is the alcoholic. There is the situation where both adults are alcoholic. There is the situation where one or more children are alcoholic. There is the situation where one or both parents are alcoholic. There is the situation where a brother or sister is the alcoholic. There is the situation where a lover and/or roommate or the roommate's lover is the alcoholic. There is the situation where the boss is the alcoholic. There is the situation where the wife of an alcoholic is trying to maintain a career. There is the situation where the child has left home physically, but not emotionally. And since alcoholism tends to run in families, and since people tend to marry people like those they have known, it is not unusual for the wife of an alcoholic to also be the daughter of an alcoholic, and for her brother or sister to also be an alcoholic, and so on and so on.

Picking only one model also leaves out other complicating variables such as chronic illness, divorce, widowhood, aging dependents, and so on, ad infinitum. The combinations become infinite, the problems too complex to deal with until they are broken down. That is why I have chosen a rather simple model to explore.

Each of the situations described above has its own special needs that cannot be minimized. Just shifting the glass does not mean that nothing else changes. However, many of the generalizations discussed in this book will work regardless of your particular situation. Because it is not outlined precisely as it affects you, does not mean that the principle does not apply.

If you are the husband or the working wife, bear in mind that compulsive overinvolvement in activity at one stage, and almost indolence at another, applies regardless of whether you are running General Motors or scrubbing the kitchen floor.

If you are a child reading this book, it should give you a better understanding of what has happened to you and how it has happened. It should also give you some idea of how you can help yourself to get out of the situation. If you are a child of one alcoholic parent, it might be a good idea to give a copy of this book to your sober parent. If you do not have a sober parent, it may be time to start looking for an adult whom you can trust. If you can't do that for yourself, write me in care of the publisher and we'll find you a way.

If you are a parent reading this book, you will probably go all through it and understand what relates to you and what you should do, and you will close the book and say, "But God help me, it's my kid—there's got to be something more I can do. If I had not been a failure as a parent, this would not have happened." It is so hard to step away from our children and see them make mistakes in their lives, regardless of whether they are ten or fifty.

I suggest to you that you read everything you can on the disease of alcoholism. Look at your extended family to see if alcoholism is part of a family trend. Until you can begin to accept the fact that you did not cause your child's disease, you cannot be of any help. You will only beat yourself into the ground and you will accomplish nothing. Worse than that—you will close off the lines of communication because your child will be unable to handle the pain he/she sees in your eyes.

If your boss is the alcoholic, you may want to take a good hard look at whether or not you are willing to work in that situation. You will be working with someone who will undermine your self-confidence, and, when you are scrambling to get your act together, will criticize you for not being more aggressive. This book should give you an understanding of what is happening. Only you can estimate the damage that can be done to you. You may decide to use it to your advantage, but I've never known anyone to outmanipulate an alcoholic until the final stages, where the disease is apparent to everyone.

A friend of mine has an alcoholic son who is no longer drinking. He decided about six months ago to join a religious cult which very heavily brainwashes its membership until they become robotlike. Two months ago he returned home, unaffected. His mother was flabbergasted. I said, "Why be surprised? You know as well as I do that *nobody* tells an alcoholic what to think." When his mother asked him to explain this seeming miracle, he said, "I took what I liked and left the rest."

To those of you reading this book, I would simply say, "Take what you can use and leave the rest." Not everything said will apply to everyone, but at the very least, you will have a better understanding of the enemy, alcoholism, and some of the weapons used in the war against it.

It is important to realize that the enemy is alcoholism. It is important to realize that even though the book is about the alcoholic marriage, it is not a male-female issue. It is important to realize that even though the book uses the traditional female role model, it is not a liberated-unliberated female issue.

In my office, I have seen men and women, old and young, black and white, Christian and non-Christian, gay and straight, professionals and laborers, rich and poor, urban and rural, single and married, and in various combinations thereof. One of the things that I am likely to say at the first interview is, "Before you tell me what is happening, let me tell you."

The response is always the same. After the initial shock has worn off, the vocal cords once again begin to function. "How did you know?"

I know because I understand what happens to the family of an alcoholic. I know because I recognize that it is not an issue of men versus women or traditional versus untraditional lifestyles, but of the *power of the sick over the well*. This illness is a great equalizer. The people who should be stronger, or wiser, or more tuned in, fall victim just as readily as everybody else. No racism or sexism here. Alcoholism supports the Equal Rights Amendment without reservation.

This book should help to make clear when it is the illness one is reacting to and when it is the person. It is only when you can understand that difference, and not allow the sickness to take over, that you can look at whatever other issues exist.

In most instances in this book, the alcoholic spouse is he and the nonalcoholic is she. I did this for a number of reasons. The first has to do with convenience. It is simpler to write it that way than to say he or she each time it is appropriate. The second has to do with the fact that the majority of my clients have been women, and I naturally think in these terms. Although we are learning that the ratio of women to men alcoholics is more even than previously thought, there is one major difference as it relates to the family. The nonalcoholic wife will more often than not remain in the marriage, whereas, the nonalcoholic husband will leave. Therefore, there is a higher percentage of women than men who require counseling in order to learn to live healthfully within the alcoholic situation. Although my discussion is slanted toward this model, most of what I say is true regardless of sex and should be recognized as such.

I'm writing this book for all of you who live with a drunk and feel you're all alone. You're not all alone. Millions of women live with alcoholics; it's a private hell, but a public problem.

I'm writing to you and about you. You may have

picked the book up because you feel desperate. You just don't know what to do anymore. You've tried everything you can think of to get your husband to stop drinking, and nothing has worked. You've tried lecturing: "Look at what you're doing to your body. You're going to rot out your liver." That hasn't worked. After all, it's his liver. You've tried tears: "If you really loved me and the children, you wouldn't do this." That hasn't worked either. You've tried hiding the bottles, threatening to leave him, and even drinking with him. You've tried nagging, reminding him about his behavior so that he won't repeat it. You tell him on the way to the party what you expect of him. He promises he won't get drunk, but he does anyway. Nothing works.

And what do you accomplish? Well you induce a little guilt; he can then drown his guilt in booze. Or you make him angry. Who wouldn't drink if he were married to you? Heads the bottle wins—tails you lose. You lose because he still drinks, and you lose because you can't stand the person you are turning into. You never imagined you would become a screaming fishwife or a tearful doormat.

Despite all of the above, I still have the nerve to say that you can learn to live with an alcoholic. Not only can you live with an alcoholic, you can be happy and productive no matter what he does. Perhaps you don't believe me. I wouldn't if I were in your place. I'd be thinking, "What does she know? If she lived with what I live with, she wouldn't hand me that crap!" Well, I *do* know how you can improve your life. Decide whether you want to try it out. If you don't, you can keep all your unhappiness. The choice is yours.

A Look at the
Problem

We live in a society where drinking alcoholic beverages is encouraged and even expected. A man has difficulty being socially "with it" when ordering club soda or a Coke. "Drinking someone under the table" is manly, and making a martini without "bruising the gin" (whatever that means) is chic. We admire the gourmet who knows the appropriate wine to drink with each course at dinner. And we laugh at the man with the lampshade on his head—unless, of course, he happens to belong to us.

Yet, the very men who are so "in" socially are "out" if they become addicted. We treat them as social outcasts and avoid them as if mere contact will taint us. They become social lepers, and so do their wives. We've all heard friends say, "I'd love to have Sally over, but you know how obnoxious Bill gets when he has a few."

You know what that feels like. You don't really want to go with him, but you don't want to go without him either. Avoiding the issue seems to be the best course to take; as a result, you don't go out at all. No one has been honest about what the problem is. If it is not discussed, you think, it will go away. But the pain of the rejection does not go away—it hurts. It hurts like hell and you are angry. Furthermore, somewhere mixed in with all those feelings is the nagging thought that somehow you are responsible. Maybe you are all those terrible things he says you are. Maybe if you were a better person, he would stop drinking. At the very least, maybe there is something that you haven't thought of that will make him stop.

The alcoholic husband of a friend of mine used to say to her, "You're such a great social worker. You help so many people. Why can't you help me?" She tried. And she believed that she should help him. She knew in her head that a doctor should not treat his own family. But in her gut, she felt extremely guilty—he knew how to make her feel that way. Yet she couldn't help him stop drinking. She was not the cause and she could not be the cure!

She was not the cause because he is an alcoholic. Alcoholism is a noncommunicable disease. No one can cause such a disease in another person.

You're probably thinking: Yeah, alcoholism is a disease and all that, but how do I know if my husband really is an alcoholic? Maybe he is just a bastard. Or morally weak, or emotionally ill, or under so much pressure that he needs the alcohol to slow down. "I *knew* that my husband could *not* be an alcoholic for a number of very good reasons," Wendy R. told me. "He was obviously not a bum. He was always well-dressed and always looked terrific. I would look like death warmed over after an all-night brawl, but he looked just fine. He held a very responsible job. He was an executive in a company where he had to make split-second decisions without wavering. His work was brilliant and everything he did won an award. Alcoholics cannot do such things. Everyone knows that there is brain damage; the brain slows down and the thinking processes get numbed. I knew he could not be an alcoholic, because it would mean that my mother was right: I should have married the other guy. I knew he could not be an alcoholic, because he never fooled around with other women and alcoholics are unfaithful."

One myth after another. "Essentially, I knew he wasn't alcoholic because I loved him, and he was my husband, and the father of my children, and *I didn't want him to be!*"

You know what? He is. He was, and is, and always will be. He has a disease called alcoholism, which is incurable. It can be arrested, but he will be an alcoholic all his life. It is a fact of his life—and hers—just as if he had diabetes or blue eyes.

I know that you are still not convinced. That's not important right now because you are thinking about the problem. The point is: No woman who has consulted me about her husband's drinking has ever been wrong. No woman ever says, "I think my husband has a drinking problem," when it's not a fact. More often than not, she has underestimated the seriousness of his drinking. Many a husband says, "She doesn't know what the hell she's talking about. I may have one or two to relax, but that's it." The amount of liquor in the one or two is, of course, not discussed. Winning the argument is not the same as winning the battle.

Alcoholics Anonymous says that if alcohol is interfering with any area of a person's life, chances are that person is an alcoholic. You had probably already decided that alcohol is having a bad effect on your life when you picked up this book. Certainly, you can agree that a problem exists. But you still don't know exactly what an alcoholic is.

As in most things, what is true for one person is not necessarily true for another. Yes, it is true that some alcoholics end up on Skid Row. Not all, but some. It is true that some alcoholics show the effects of the chemical in their physical appearance. Some alcoholics cannot hold a job of any nature. Even some mothers are right! Not Wendy's, though. Wendy married Jim because she was very much in love and, in spite of all her troubles, she would do it again. If you attend an AA meeting, you will meet all kinds of people from every walk of life. Just as in any other group of people, you will be drawn to some and others will turn you off. The main things these people have in common are their alcoholism and their desire to come to grips with the disease.

The only statement that applies to all alcoholics is that an alcoholic is a person who cannot drink normally. There is, however, a cluster of personality traits that most alcoholics have in common. Although not every alcoholic has all of these traits, and they are not exclusive to alcoholics, some knowledge of them will help you to understand what is happening to him, and you, and to those around you. What happens is predictable. Knowing this may make you feel less alone. Later we will talk about what you can do about your situation—what you can do so that you can enjoy your life and enjoy being you. The alcoholic's traits that I am going to discuss include: (a) excessive dependency; (b) emotional immaturity; (c) low frustration tolerance; (d) inability to express emotions; (e) high level of anxiety in interpersonal relationships; (f) low self-esteem; (g) grandiosity; (h) feelings of isolation; (i) perfectionism; (j) ambivalence toward authority; and (k) guilt.

Excessive Dependency

The alcoholic is a very dependent person. He prefers not to take responsibility for his behavior. Let George do it. Then when George does it, if anything goes wrong, it's George's fault. He himself would not have made the mistake. The alcoholic prefers to have someone make all his decisions for him, including what he eats and what he wears. Recently, I've been working with a family in which the alcoholic husband is continually threatening suicide. This keeps the rest of the family off balance. Every time he makes his threat, they get scared and try to talk him out of it. They minister to his every need and whim. This man cannot decide whether to have cornflakes or an egg for breakfast, and quite often, he eats nothing.

The last time his wife called me in a panic with "This time he really means it," I answered, "Say good-bye. After all, if he really means it, there's nothing you can do." When she said "Good-bye" he came right home. What else could he do? Thinking he might be ready for some help, I called him the next day. "My family would be better off without me," he lamented. "They probably won't dance in the streets," I answered, "but I will, because at least you have made a decision." I also gave him the name of a doctor who would prescribe medication to ease convulsions while he was making his decision. He still hasn't made it.

He's dying more slowly from alcohol than from the more flamboyant act of suicide, but he's given up the threats. His wife and two oldest daughters started college this fall. One of them is a student of mine and comes in smiling and happy. They are my main interest. They have not abandoned their alcoholic, but they have learned how not to abandon themselves either. He's not too crazy about me because he can't control them anymore. Yet, he still does not want to take responsibility for his behavior.

Avoiding responsibility and making decisions is one of the things that causes alcoholics to drink at first. But drinking does not resolve dependency problems. The alcohol itself becomes a need. His "I just need a drink to relax me so I can think clearly" becomes a vicious cycle, creating even worse physical and emotional dependency.

Emotional Immaturity

"When an individual starts drinking alcoholically, he stops developing emotionally" is a common maxim. He just looks like forty. Emotionally he is about seventeen. I'm sure you often feel that your alcoholic husband is just another child in the house. This, as strange as it may sound, is very close to the truth. A client of mine was making wonderful progress, which stopped suddenly. After a month had passed, I finally confronted him. Was there a change in his life that was getting in his way? The only thing he could think of was taking two or three drinks each night in order to get to sleep. Those two or three drinks could have been shot glasses or tumblers. From the moment he started drinking to excess, he stopped developing emotionally. My position was quite clear: I do not counsel chemicals. When he eliminated the alcohol, we were able to move on.

Emotional growth tends to result from confronting discomfort or pain. If we remember clearly, we have to admit that the times we grew the most were during times of trial. The happy times, the carefree times, were not growing times. I have never heard anyone say, "It was a wonderful easygoing time, and boy did I grow." Growth seems to come with a desire to develop or change, along with a discomfort about things the way they are. Since the alcoholic is busy anesthetizing himself against unpleasant reality, he cannot develop emotionally. His chronological age and his emotional age are very different. One is adult and the other, child. You get into trouble when you expect this drunk child to act like a sober adult. How many times have you criticized your alcoholic husband for his behavior? You were, in effect, asking a drunk to act sober when you said, "Don't drive like that!" If you had in you what he had in him, would you drive any differently? Probably worse. "Don't cry like that!" we say to a child. He replies, "It's the only way I know how to cry!" What we are really saying to the child is, "Don't cry!" and what we are really saying to the alcoholic is, "Don't be drunk!" That's a contradiction in terms. It is natural for the child to cry, and it is natural for the alcoholic to drink.

Low Frustration Tolerance

The alcoholic has a short fuse, and you never really know what particular thing is going to set it off. Life itself ignites the fuse. Certainly a wife and children get in the way. The least little thing can set your husband off. Things tend to happen which cause outrageous reactions. The phone has a habit of ringing when someone calls. Alcoholics have been known to rip it off the wall because it has the nerve to intrude. In addition, a simple snag can turn the whole day into a nightmare— the babysitter is ten minutes late, there is no clean towel in the bathroom, or the mayonnaise is on the wrong piece of bread.

The ordinary frustrations of everyday living are overwhelming to the alcoholic. Have you ever noticed the way children walk through a room, and it immediately looks like a disaster area? They *really* didn't do anything. I'm constantly amazed! Nobody did anything, but the time I spend cleaning up the kitchen that nobody had anything to eat in, defies the imagination. The alcoholic cannot handle this kind of frustration. He wants things the way he wants them, when he wants them, and how he wants them. If it doesn't work his way, he either becomes violent and busts up the place before storming out to drink, or, if he is not prone to violence, he simply takes refuge in drink. It is a way, if only temporarily, to dull the nerve endings. Since the frustrations he is unable to handle are not the ones that go away, he invariably has reason to get drunk again.

As a result of your husband's irrational behavior, you

start to walk on eggs. You don't want to set him off, so you are very careful not to do or say the wrong thing. You also try to get the children to be very careful about what they do and say. You look for the "right" time to tell him about the dentist bill. You become tense trying to keep everything calm, and then something happens to screw it up anyway: The car won't start; a light bulb blows; somebody forgot to put the cap back on the toothpaste. It is all your fault because you are a rotten wife, or a rotten mother, or a rotten housekeeper. The abuse varies according to the particular drunk, but it does go on and on.

If you're like most people, you can't help thinking that in some way it was your fault. You could have checked the toothpaste; you did have a hard time starting the car yesterday; and if you had only. . . . What you are not allowing for is the fact that if it wasn't the toothpaste, or the car, it would have been that you talk too much, or you don't talk enough—but it would have been something. It's hard at the time to think logically, because while you are taking responsibility for whatever he is frustrated and angry about, you are also feeling things like, "No jury in the world would convict me of manslaughter if they knew him." And then since nice people don't commit murder, or even think about it, you feel guilty. You've lost again.

Inability to Express Emotions

The alcoholic is unable to talk about what he is feeling and keeps his feelings "bottled" up. (Forgive the pun. I couldn't resist.) One of the things alcohol does is disinhibit. It makes us feel freer to say and do things that we might not ordinarily say and do. For example, a man who is usually very shy and withdrawn can become very charming and popular after a couple of drinks. This is what happens in the beginning. As the drinking goes on, a couple of other things happen. Repressed feelings start to emerge. And perception of reality is distorted. That means purple cows and pink elephants.

Emotions are not properly directed either. Since the alcohol distorts perception, the emotions expressed are not necessarily appropriate to the situation. More often than not, the feelings expressed toward others are antagonistic. These feelings are actually feelings that the alcoholic has about himself, but which are too painful to deal with, even under the influence of alcohol. Talking about how you feel can take the edge off, but resolving these feelings takes work. The alcoholic goes no further than blowing off steam or dumping his feelings on others. That is, if the feelings he has kept in are feelings of anger, he will behave in an angry manner. But the person he is really angry at is himself. Because he cannot face the fact, he will let you have it.

Whether you believe him or not, you listen and are terribly hurt. You don't realize that even though he is talking to you, he is mainly talking about himself. He is filled with self hate. "Can someone lie when he is drunk?" I am often asked. "I don't know," I reply. "It doesn't really matter." Since the alcoholic's perceptions are distorted, he may be lying when he thinks he is telling the truth. And telling the truth when he thinks he is lying. Even if what he says is true, you can only believe it for the moment that he is saying it anyway. An alcoholic once told me, "I've lived a lie for so long, I don't know what truth is." *That* I could believe!

We live in a society where it is not considered manly to cry, to be afraid or insecure, to show any of the frail-ties that make us human. If a man feels these things, he certainly doesn't want to admit them—even to himself. Thus, if he feels these things and has even more diffi-culty expressing feelings because he is an alcoholic, he turns to the bottle and exposes his flip side. I have often wondered if *Dr. Jekyll and Mr. Hyde* was modeled after an alcoholic. I would not be at all surprised, because this book so clearly describes much of what we see in the alcoholic personality. "When he is drunk, he is not the person I married," many women have told me. "I don't know him at all. He is a stranger to me." My response is something terribly profound like, "He doesn't seem like the man you married, because he is not the man you married." That is the reality of the situation.

High Level of Anxiety in Interpersonal Relationships

Alcoholics tend not to make friends easily. They suffer from feelings of inferiority. They have trouble relating to others for fear of being found out. They don't want people to see beyond the facade of normalcy. As a result, they establish short- rather than long-term friendships, and when the friendships start to get close, they end them or become less available. They do, however, have drinking buddies and believe these people are their friends.

When an alcoholic is drinking, he is able to forget his fears and, at least to himself, feel in control. Alcoholics can be very cunning, very charming, and very manipulative. I guess I don't have to tell you about that. You have fallen victim to your husband's charms over and over, only to be shattered when his personality changes. Perhaps he has convinced you that this time, he really means it. He'll give the alcohol up. He loves you. And, of course, he can't give it up. You fall for his story every time, as he is exceedingly clever. And you want so badly to believe him. This time it will be different. You think. How vulnerable and trusting you are.

You are not the only one who succumbs. He cons his boss—for a while. He cons those he borrows money from—for a while. He cons the police and the courts. You have to be very careful when you take him to court that you don't end up with egg on your face. How could this good-looking, charming man have thrown you down the stairs in a drunken rage? Even if he admits it, the judge is assured it will never happen again. Boys will be boys.

When your alcoholic husband has difficulty with interpersonal relationships, except at a distance, you will find that your friendships with other couples drop off. As the disease progresses, you will be spending less and less time with people you used to be close to. There are a number of reasons for this. One of them is he just cannot handle the closeness. He will make excuses or decide he doesn't like them. He is simply too uncomfortable in a social situation. He will probably be all right if you push him into accepting an invitation by saying when he gets there he can have a few drinks, but the idea of going at all is very frightening to him. You will be hurt because you cannot continue your friendships very long under this kind of pressure. The truth is, sadly enough, that there is no way to maintain a couple-to-couple friendship with only half a couple. It is too unfair, and too hard, to make the other couple understand, especially when you are protecting him, covering up for the real problem. A cover-up usually sounds like a cover-up, no matter how convincing you try to be.

Low Self-Esteem

Alcoholics generally have very little sense of self-worth. They do not see themselves as people of value. The alcohol gives them a false sense of self-confidence, an "I can do anything!" attitude. This false sense of self-confidence then gives way to the outrageous. I'm sure you've heard alcoholics claim that they can do just about anything. There is no problem too big for them to handle. The presidency is small potatoes. The next day, if they remember their claims, they feel embarrassed, guilty, and remorseful. Since they do not think much of themselves to begin with, their behavior while drunk reinforces their negative self-image. The reasoning goes: A person who is worth something does not behave like that. If I were not a terrible person, I would not have done that. I am just a crumb.

If you're honest enough to admit it, you probably support your husband's feelings of inferiority. When there is any part of that evening he does not remember, you are right there to remind him: "How could you have said that to her? How could you have made a pass at my best friend? Do you think they *really* thought that story was funny?" His inner feelings that he is worthless are, again, reinforced. Since this is a very painful reality, and he runs away from painful realities, he returns to the bottle. And you are flabbergasted. You thought that after the performance he put on last night and the amount of liquor he consumed, if you weren't lucky enough to have him hit by a Mack truck, at least he would give up drinking. Not so. Foiled again. The disease beat you. It always will. Face it, he is powerless over alcohol—and so are you.

Grandiosity

I once heard an alcoholic defined as an egomaniac with an inferiority complex. As the alcoholic drinks, this insecure person becomes more and more flamboyant. He goes from Harry, to Mr. Harry, to Sir Harry, to the ruler of the universe. His grandiosity is limitless. He is the king. And don't you forget it. He is also living in a fantasy world. My four-year-old just left the house dressed as Superman, although he believes he is Superman less now than he did at age two. When he was two, he tried to fly and chipped his tooth. Now he knows he is playing a game. I'm not so sure that the alcoholic knows he is playing a game. The chemical changes the character, and lo and behold—as one alcoholic described himself—KING BABY!

Grandiose behavior is not limited to verbal obnoxiousness. The grandiose alcoholic thinks nothing of ordering all new furniture for the living room or a newer and bigger car. Paying for it is not a problem, because his fantasy includes making a lot of money. When he takes you out, he feels free to shout, "This round's on me!" I know one woman who had all she could do to keep from getting completely hysterical when her husband paid for the dinner eaten by the couple at the next table. This incident occurred after she had spent the day hunting for shoes at bargain prices for her children. The wife, as she watches the paycheck fly by, is ignored if she objects with decorum, and considered a shrew if she makes a scene. After all, he is just being generous. The promotion is just around the corner. Being poor is a state of mind. There is no limit to the amount of money that an alcoholic with grandiose tendencies can spend. In effect, he is trying to buy respect and friendship. He has nothing left of himself to give. But the momentary elation and applause soon fade and the broken pieces follow. The family literally pays the price.

Feelings of Isolation

It has often been said that we can love others only to the degree that we love ourselves. If this is true, and I suspect it is, then the alcoholic is unable to offer love.

When one is unable to show love, it becomes more and more difficult to receive love. The love his family gives him makes the alcoholic feel guilty. And because he feels undeserving of love, he retreats to the bottle. His companions at the bar give him a false sense of camaraderie for a while, but that quickly fades as his drinking progresses. He is locked into himself.

As the disease progresses, the isolation he feels takes on another form. People turn away from him. Friends refuse to see him. His family goes the other way when he comes home. He may lose his job. Even his friend, the bartender, may refuse to serve him. The isolation becomes a reality. He is truly alone. In his desperation, he turns to his only true friend—the bottle. What a self-feeding disease this is! The alcoholism causes the changes that bring about the excruciating loneliness— and then it offers itself as the only way out.

You watch and feel cut off and lonely too. You start to wonder if you wouldn't feel less lonely than you are now, if you were completely without him. You, too, have become isolated from most of your social contacts, and it's hard to imagine yourself going out and meeting new people, making new friends and being desirable. And you don't even have the bottle for solace. Your pain is raw. Joan L. admitted to me that she ate chocolate to push down those nagging feelings. "The cake wouldn't even have to be thawed out for me to go at it," she said. "I would stuff myself to the point where I was nauseous, and that feeling would prevail over the loneliness." The family can indeed become sicker than the alcoholic. I don't know about you, but Joan was well on her way. If you think about it, you can probably top that story with the crazy stuff you've done.

Perfectionism

The alcoholic is a perfectionist. He cannot tolerate lack of perfection in himself, or in others. Working with him is almost impossible, because there is no way to meet his standards. Any project he undertakes has to be done perfectly. If he cannot do it perfectly, he may not do it at all. Yet when he makes the attempt, he takes so much time doing it, that it is hardly worth having it done. "He bought the paint, the brushes, and the drop cloth and prepared the room for painting," Barbara told me. "Two-and-a-half years later, I decided I had better do it myself." Perfectionism, coupled with low frustration tolerance, becomes an excuse to abandon the project and drink. This particular mixture is very explosive, and the family is well-advised to keep their distance.

You may be thinking I have described a lot of people you know—that perfectionism is not peculiar to the alcoholic. You are probably right. However, the inability to find an effective way of dealing with the frustration caused by the need to be perfect, is what makes the alcoholic different. In a more typical personality, these feelings are manageable. They blow over, or after a brief outburst the crisis is over. The alcoholic's reactions are all out of proportion to the situation, and they give him an excuse to drink.

You are constantly left with the questions, "Do I wait until he does it, or do I get it done myself? I have no doubts that he will do it better, but by the time he gets around to it will I be too old to enjoy it?" Eight months ago, an alcoholic I know bought a game that hooks up to the television set. He is waiting for just the right moment to attach it. His oldest child is a sophomore in high school, and I have a feeling that the right moment will not arrive before the boy goes off to college. Periodically, his wife suggests he hook the game up. He gets angry and defensive, but they still wait.

The situation above is not very serious. But those of you who have lived with the water turned off for the weekend because your husband was going to fix the plumbing himself, and then it turned out he didn't have the exact wrench he needed, know what I am talking about. "It's a simple job," he says. "Nothing to it!" Those fateful words. And you end up using the neighbor's bathroom, trying to make light of the fact that you want to hit your husband over the head with a sledge hammer. You know you'll end up calling the plumber anyway, because in the middle of the job, he will take off and get drunk because the blankety blank something or other won't fit into the blankety blank something.

If he gets through the whole job, it will probably be wonderful. You will, however, have to convince yourself it was worth it. Those gray hairs do not stop appearing. If you tell the story, people will have a good laugh. But you may have to wait five years until it seems funny to you. Pamela L. waited three years for her husband to replace the fallen ceiling in her kitchen. She was determined to wait it out. Her husband called me one day to come over and take a look at the lovely new ceiling. He's very proud of himself. The ceiling looks wonderful—but *three* years! If I were writing for any group of people other than you who are married to alcoholics, most of what I am saying would not be believed. You know that I am not making anything up. I'm just telling it the way it is.

Ambivalence Toward Authority

Authority figures mean nothing to the alcoholic who is drinking. He has the same reactions as you or I when he is sober, but when he is drinking nobody is going to tell him what to do. He doesn't concern himself with the illegality of speeding or hit-and-run driving. The problem is compounded by the police, who tend to be much more sympathetic with alcohol abusers than with drug abusers. I observed an instance in which an alcoholic had been picked up for a hit-and-run collision. He was obviously smashed. But he was charming. The charm of the alcoholic is not to be underestimated. He was so charming that the police refused, over the protests of the man he had hit, to give him a drunkometer test. His wife, Brenda, kept her mouth shut. Enablers all! He got some points on his license, but this sick man was allowed to go back out there on the streets where the next time he might kill himself or somebody else. Sometimes being the nice guy is not the nice thing to do. No wonder the alcoholic is ambivalent. The authorities are ambivalent. I talked to his wife later. She said she simply lacked courage. After worrying all night she was so relieved that he was still in one piece, she just sat down and shook. Brenda would not react that way today because she knows she aided and abetted alcoholism that night. She didn't know any better. You will—so that when it happens to you—and it will—you will have a choice.

There is humor in everything, if we allow ourselves to see it. The only concern Brenda's husband had during the ordeal was that he shouldn't lose his keys. Not a thought about her, the other people involved, or the damage to his car. After what seemed like forever, he and Brenda got home. He went up to bed and she, unable to sleep, went into the den. Soon the doorbell rang. It was the police. Yes, he had remembered his keys, but he had also picked up the keys to their patrol car. They wondered if she would be so kind as to return them. Even though they told her she had the right to remain silent, she continued to laugh as they meekly walked out to the street with the keys that her husband had not forgotten.

Guilt

Guilt is a mainstay in the alcoholic home. The alcoholic is terribly guilt-ridden. He does not want to behave the way that he does, and he does not like the person he is when he is drunk. He doesn't understand that he has no control over his behavior when he is drunk. He promises, because he really loves his family and wants to keep his job, that he will stop drinking. He is not lying. He really means it when he says it. But he does not have a choice. So he disappoints himself and everyone who cares about him or needs him. This makes him feel very guilty. Unable to confront the pain he must ease it, and consequently he drinks some more. This makes him feel even more guilty. Then you feel guilty because of the part you play in making him feel guilty and he feels yet guiltier . . . and once again the bottle wins. He gets sicker and sicker and *you get sicker and sicker*!

These traits I've discussed are not true for all alcoholics, nor does any one alcoholic necessarily possess all of them. Nor are these traits exclusive to alcoholics. They are, however, traits that alcoholics seem to exhibit with far greater frequency than more typical populations.

What Happens
to You

You cannot live with active alcoholism without being profoundly affected. Any human being who is bombarded with what you've been bombarded with is to be commended for sheer survival. You deserve a medal for the mere fact that you're around to tell the story. I know it has not been easy. You don't know from day to day—even hour to hour—what to expect. You imagine all kinds of terrible things and, as often as not, you are right. You become obsessed with what will happen when he gets home (if he gets home). Your day is spent in emotional turmoil. Your head keeps spinning. You can't sleep. You don't eat properly. You look terrible. You withdraw from your friends. You snap at your children.

You're sick. You have developed a disease which we call near-alcoholism, which is every bit as damaging as alcoholism itself. Like alcoholism it has its own symptoms. Anyone who has close contact with an alcoholic is affected by the disease, the degree being directly related to one's emotional nearness. Since you have the most continual and relevant contact with your husband, you are the most vulnerable.

As there are some patterns which described the alcoholic's behavior, there are also some patterns in your responses. No one close to an alcoholic escapes responding in at least some of the ways I will discuss. It is only a matter of degree. The following are the symptoms of near-alcoholism: denial; protectiveness, pity/concern

29

about the drinker; embarrassment, avoiding drinking occasions; shift in relationship; guilt; obsession, continual worry; fear; lying; false hope, disappointment, euphoria; confusion; sex problems; anger; lethargy, hopelessness, self-pity, remorse and despair. As you read about these symptoms, try to identify the ones you have. Recognizing a problem is the first step in getting rid of it.

Denial

Denial is your biggest enemy. It seems impossible to believe that you are involved with an alcoholic. It simply cannot be true. If it cannot be true, it isn't true. You believe what you want to believe. You ignore reality. Because the alcoholic wants to face reality even less than you do, he helps you to be unrealistic. Denial is part of the disease for both you and your husband. He expends a great deal of energy denying the fact that he cannot control his drinking. He seems to control it for long periods of time. These periods grow shorter as the disease progresses, but he will convince both you and himself that he is the master of the bottle. Pure fantasy! The alcoholic does not seek help until he can no longer deny his lack of control and until the results of his behavior have been so horrifying he feels the pain despite the drug.

You don't look at the problem honestly either. You don't

seek help until you are overwhelmed by fear of violence, loss of income, and uncertainty about what each day will bring. As the disease progresses, you take over more and more of the family responsibility. You try to maintain control over the situation and act as if everything is manageable. You deny the turmoil that exists within, as well as without, because denial is the most tolerable way to cope with an otherwise intolerable situation.

You go around in circles until the denial no longer works. You have no choice but to face facts when the weight of the evidence is overwhelming, and the pain is too great to handle. Denial is part of the process that enables the disease to progress. This is true of any disease. How many unnecessary deaths have there been because people would not, for example, accept the fact that they had cancer? Disease flourishes in the virus of denial.

In order to combat near-alcoholism, you must first admit that the problem exists. I say that glibly, but I know how hard it is. Cindy M. takes a hard look at herself: "I was one of the most skillful deniers around. I just couldn't admit there was a problem. I just couldn't let go of the idea that I could figure out a way to make it disappear just like a bad dream. I denied in the face of the undeniable.

"My husband had a drinking problem before we were married," Cindy relates. "Every time I broke off with him, it was as a result of a drunken episode. I discounted those episodes because I loved him. I discounted them until about five years ago when there was nothing else I could do. That was thirteen years into the marriage. I made excuses for him. The pressures at work were incredible, and he needed a few drinks in order to unwind. Made perfect sense. I would even mix his drinks for him. He complained about the job and went over and over the same story, never reaching a solution. I would sit with him very sympathetically. I always got to bed later than was good for me, but after all, he needed me.

"I denied that the problem was alcohol. It's hard to believe how naive I was. When I tried to go to bed, he would wake me up. I'd get up rather than risk waking the children. Night after night this went on. I told no one. Who could I trust? I had created the image of the ideal couple and didn't want that damaged. And I didn't want anyone to think less of him.

"He started getting violent. With one stroke of his arm he could clear the kitchen table or break everything on a shelf. Then I'd stay up most of the night picking up the broken glass and scrubbing the mustard off the walls. I didn't want the children to find it when they woke up in the morning. They had to be protected.

"My mother started nagging me that my skin looked bad and my house wasn't clean. But I didn't tell. What could she do anyway? I was afraid of an 'I told you so.'

"Deny, deny, deny. I was seven months pregnant when I landed in the emergency room to get my arm stitched up. He threw a glass at me when I wouldn't get out of bed at two in the morning to talk to him. He threw it with such force that it shattered. I covered for him. I protected him. I denied. I just couldn't face the truth.

"I denied until I could deny no more. The neighbors saw him staggering home. Who was I fooling? My mother spent a night with me. Why had I shut her out? My children knew something was terribly wrong. I had accomplished nothing. I simply couldn't face up to what was happening until I had no choice. My stubbornness only made it worse. My seeming strength was really only lack of courage. My ignorance was appalling. The person I am today would have behaved very differently. The person I am today demands the right to her personhood. Reality must be dealt with. Pretending it doesn't exist does not make it go away. I learned that the hard way."

That's an example of what denial can do to a person. I gave you Cindy's story. It could have been Barbara's or Joan's or Nancy's. They are all variations on the same theme. Denial makes life a lie. It distorts reality every bit as much for the nonalcoholic as the alcohol distorts reality for the alcoholic. If you choose to give denial up, you will experience an almost immediate sense of relief—get that monkey off your back. You can adjust to truth. You don't have to like it, but you cannot deny it and be healthy.

Protectiveness, Pity/Concern About the Drinker

In the early stages of alcoholism we are all very understanding. "Yes, dear, I know it's a jungle out there. Yes, you should have gotten the promotion. You work so hard with so little appreciation. Let me fix you a drink." You feel very sorry for your husband and his suffering. You worry about him and try to find solutions to his problems. There is no way to solve his problems, however, as he becomes more and more skillful at snatching defeat from the jaws of victory. If there is something to worry about or be angry about, he will find it. The injustice can be real or imagined. It doesn't matter.

Night after night you get sucked in and lose sight of yourself in an attempt to pacify your alcoholic. After all, he is out there bringing home the paycheck and you owe it to him to make things as smooth for him at home as you possibly can. The fact that you've had a rough day too is not important. It is part of your role to make the world right for your husband. Your needs are not important. Jean B. remembers: "That's what my husband told me. You know what else? I believed him. And more and more I became less and less. I became a servant in my own home. I had no needs. But I sure had a good case of colitis. Those feelings that I denied I had were eating my guts out. I was so concerned for my husband that I would bleed. Everything was being drained out of me. We non-persons do things like that. But not anymore."

Embarrassment, Avoiding Drinking Occasions

What other people think of us seems to be very important—far more important, in fact, than what we think of ourselves. We assume that others are judging us by our own behavior and by the behavior of those around us, especially that of our family. When I bragged about my youngest son walking at nine months, was I saying, "He's terrific," or was I saying, "I'm terrific"? By the same token, when the older kids run into trouble at school, unless I make a conscious effort to separate myself from them, I consider it a negative reflection on me as a parent. Since you are probably like most people, when your alcoholic husband behaves outrageously, you're embarrassed. You make excuses and wish you were invisible. You don't feel that you can go home, leaving the "life of the party" behind. A number of these experiences will cause you to feel insecure and afraid of social situations where there is drinking. Eventually, you want to avoid such situations altogether. The embarrassment is too great. You are, in effect, taking responsibility for his behavior. The truth is that you can really only take responsibility for your own behavior. At this point, that statement doesn't make much sense. You also don't understand that other people often don't know that your husband's behavior humiliates you. Other people's drunken husbands don't bother me. Sometimes I enjoy them because I don't have to go home with them.

You also can't enjoy the party because you're watching him all the time, suggesting that maybe he's had enough, trying to get him to leave, insisting on driving. It reaches a point where it's just not worth going in the first place. If you can't have a good time, why bother? Consequently, you feel sorry for yourself and nurse your wounds.

Shift in Relationship—Domination, Takeover, Self-Absorptive Activities

As the disease progresses, the alcoholic assumes less and less responsibility. The relationship between you and your husband and you and your children changes. You take over more and more. You try to become both mother and father to your children. This is not possible. A mother simply can not be a father. She is just not built for it. A mother can only be the best mother she is able to be. When she tries to be a father, too, she takes on an

impossible task. Not only is it unrealistic, it is destructive to the children. She causes confusion in their minds
and wears herself out.

You become more and more in charge and make vir-
tually all the decisions in the house. The alcoholic eventually becomes yet another child. And although you
dominate him as you would a child, you become angry
and resentful when he does not behave like an adult.
You're afraid that everything will fall apart if you don't
take charge. So you run the house and care for the kids;
you handle the finances, paint the walls, mow the
lawn—in effect, you do it all. You may even go to work
so you can be sure there is enough income. You are definitely in control and running the show. When I watch
women doing this, I am reminded of Joan of Arc. It
really makes you stop and think. There's not too much
satisfaction in martyrdom, not for most people anyway.

After taking over, it is not unusual for you to get
involved in lots of activities outside of the home. You are
continually busy. These self-absorptive activities are a
form of escape. Even if what you are doing is very productive, your motive is less to be helpful than to avoid
thinking. Mary N. is a highly skilled teacher specializing
in children with learning problems. She says, "I did
tutoring with neurologically impaired children at one
time. Although I did a good job, I did it more because it

afforded me a little financial independence than out of concern for the children. I would do anything in order to avoid an issue that might be potentially explosive."

Even though your outside activities may benefit others, the satisfaction to you is limited. It is limited because you are running away from, not toward, something. It also can make the situation at home more difficult to bear. On the outside, you are respected and appreciated. You forget that you will not be respected and appreciated at home. Anything that you are involved in that does not revolve around him is a threat. He is so needy, he resents any of your energy being directed elsewhere. You are never ready for his criticisms. Zapped again!

You are vulnerable. Thus you feel guilty, not only because of what your husband is doing, but because you know that you'll fight not to give up your bridge game, garden club or part-time job. A part of you knows that you are not doing such a bad thing. But just how strong is that part? Mary N. compromised: "I gave up the bridge game and kept the job. I also lied to my friends. I even forgot what I told them, but they didn't believe it and neither did I. I would not do that today. I might or might not compromise, but I know I wouldn't lie. I also know that if I chose to compromise, it would be out of a desire to accommodate and not out of fear. The *reason* for what I do is every bit as important as the thing itself. I want to act out of strength and not weakness. I want a choice, and today I have it." And you will, too.

Guilt

The alcoholic is an expert at projecting his own guilt feelings onto you. You become an expert at accepting them. When he avoids responsibility for his behavior, yelling, "You drive me to drink!" you take it on yourself.

You begin to think that if you were a better wife, he would not drink. He agrees. The children start to think that if they were better kids, he would not drink. He agrees with them, too. You tread carefully in order not to set off your alcoholic. Of course, this does not work either. One of my favorite stories involves an alcoholic who asked his dutiful wife to fix him two eggs, one sunny side up and the other over easy. When she presented him with the eggs, he refused to eat them, complaining, "You turned the wrong one!"

When you hear how terrible you are over a period of time, it is almost impossible not to believe it. As a result, much of what the alcoholic says is internalized and you become ridden with guilt. The alcoholic knows just where you are vulnerable and pushes those buttons.

Guilt is a very strong manipulative force. Gloria told me how guilt affected her: "I felt guilty because I couldn't stop my husband from drinking. I felt guilty because I couldn't always control my children's behavior. I felt guilty when I was ten minutes late getting home from a tennis lesson. I felt guilty if I played cards at night when he wanted me at home. I felt guilty for crimes I didn't understand. I found ways to apologize when I didn't know what I did, even when I was in the right. I didn't want a hassle and I couldn't stand his rejecting me when he was angry. My thinking was as off as his. The difference was that he was acting and I was reacting. He dished out the guilt and I swallowed it whole. I became so filled with guilt that I reached the point I just couldn't handle it anymore. So I gave it all up. Today my conscience tells me right from wrong, but my guilt button no longer operates. When I'm wrong I promptly admit it, but when I believe I'm right I can stand by it." You can do it, too.

Obsession, Continual Worry

As the disease occupies more and more of the alcoholic's thoughts, it has the same effect on you. Life is no longer predictable and you are continually worried. What will happen next? Will he be caught drinking on the job? Will he be fired? Where is he? Will he be home on time? Will he get hurt? Where will he go? Will he be violent? How can I get him to stop drinking? Where have I gone wrong? Is there another woman? Should I leave him? Why do I love him? Is there a way out?

These worrisome thoughts crowd out all other thoughts. You're in a squirrel cage. You go through the motions of living, but your mind is elsewhere—always on the alcoholic. This obsession is a waste of energy because it solves nothing. It only makes the whole family sicker, more involved in the emotional orbit of your husband. Knowing this does not help much. You are trapped. You have lost control of your thoughts and life is a nightmare. After several weeks in counseling Linda B. confided, "I remember driving past a cemetery and feeling envy. I saw a funeral procession and thought, *At least* he's *got friends*. That's the pit of despair and the height of self-pity. The one advantage to feeling that low is that if you choose to go on, there is no place to go but up. I don't ever want to feel that way again. I will never allow that to happen." And you don't have to either.

Fear

Anxiety and fear are usually present in the alcoholic home. Some of these fears are groundless, and some are well-founded, such as: Can I make it alone? Will he beat me? What if he loses his job? I know a woman whose husband chained the doors when she left the house so she couldn't get back in. At first she was afraid to leave because the thought of being locked out with her children locked in terrified her. Later on, she learned to carry a screwdriver and undo the latch. Her fear, once confronted, was manageable.

Charlotte S. describes her fear: "I found that most of the things I was afraid of happened. I also found that I was anxious much of the time, but couldn't figure out why. If I ate lunch and the feeling went away, it was hunger; if it didn't, it was anxiety. Fear became a way of life for me. I hid it well from outsiders, but my stomach knew. I found that the time and energy I spent being afraid was not good for me, so I tried to put my energies elsewhere for as long as I could. When I was attending classes, I found that I was in a panic on the way to school. After all, I was leaving my three children behind—with him. I was nauseous during class, and then I would race home. I would travel an hour each way to hear a man I respected, and my head would be elsewhere. Four wasted hours! With that awareness came a commitment to myself; I decided to be where I was at the moment. I could not change what was happening at home, but I *could* decide whether to waste my time where I was or to concentrate and get something out of it. It was hard work, but I won."

Many women lose confidence in themselves as a result of living with an alcoholic. Then they become very fearful and anxious. Situations that at one time were not at all threatening become overwhelming. These women become more and more the victims of their nameless fears. I know some women living with active alcoholics who are terrified of being alone, others who are afraid to leave the house. They can't explain why, but the fear overwhelms them. It's terrible to live in fear. It renders us immobile. It makes us behave in irrational ways. One act out of fear leads to another, and we lose control of our lives. We start spinning our wheels with no place to go.

Lying

Lying is a way of life in the alcoholic home. You lie in order to protect the alcoholic. You tell his boss, "I'm sorry, he won't be in to work today. He has the flu." You explain to your neighbor, "I don't know how the lamp got broken. The cat must have knocked it over."

The alcoholic lies to you, his boss and himself, saying such things as, "I have no liquor in the house." "I had only one beer." I know of one alcoholic who had thirty-five members of his family die in three years. Some of the same people died two or three times. He missed many days of work with the excuse that he had to attend a funeral.

The most destructive of all are the lies that are not really lies. They are truthful in intent, but not in execution. The alcoholic says, "I will be home at 6:00 for dinner!" He is not lying. He fully intends to be home at 6:00 for dinner. But he does not arrive home at 6:00, because there is a world of difference between his intent and his ability to carry it out. He tells the children he will take them to the ball game on Saturday. He means it when he says it. When Saturday comes, he is passed out on the floor. What is a lie? What is the truth? Who is responsible?

This kind of behavior adds greatly to the confusion and disorganization of your family. Truth loses its meaning, and perceptions of reality become distorted. You simply do not know what to believe. In the end, you believe pretty much what you want to believe. This leads to continually setting yourself up for a letdown. He is so convincing, and you would rather believe him than the evidence of last week's burnt dinner or unused theater tickets. That can all change, however. You can learn to eat and go to the theater alone if you have to. But you have to get well first.

False Hope, Disappointment, Euphoria

Part of what throws the alcoholic's family into confusion and despair is the building up of hopes and the subsequent disappointment. The family, unable to accept reality, lives in fantasy. You think of your alcoholic husband in terms of what he was or could be. When he makes a promise you respond as if he were that person. When he does not fulfill his promise, you are let down much more than you would be if you had not believed him in the first place. If he does keep his promise, you are so excited you become euphoric. This, of course, sets you up for greater disappointment the next time. The alternating feelings of false hope, disappointment, and euphoria add to your confusion and fear.

You have, in effect, given him control over your happiness. He now has the power to make you happy or miserable. He uses and abuses this power as a way of manipulating you. If you do not behave according to his desires, he will not take you to the party. If he has decided ahead of time that he wants a way out, there is nothing you can do. He sometimes withholds his manipulative moves until the very last minute. And there you are all dressed up with no place to go.

You really believed that *this* time he would follow through. You were getting along so well. He hadn't had a drink in two weeks. *This time it would be different.* How many times have you said those words to yourself? How many times has the alcoholic said those words to himself? Yes, it's different. It's worse. The disease progresses. You are not in control. Your husband is not really in control. The alcohol is in control—if you allow it to be.

Confusion

You become confused when you live with an alcoholic. You don't know what to believe or what to expect. Since he is pulling the strings, you are dancing to a very incon-sistent tune. Your sense of what is real becomes distorted. Every day is more unmanageable, a living nightmare.

In your confusion you may decide that you will drink with your husband. Having tried everything else you could think of, you decide, "If I can't lick him, I'll join him." You think that maybe this way he will cut down or become less abusive. The results are predictable. You can't keep up with him. If your children see you drink-ing with their father, they become even more fearful and confused. They think that their mother, too, will become an alcoholic. Thus everyone gets sucked a little deeper into the alcoholic abyss.

It is very hard for you to think straight. In fact, it is very hard for you to think at all. You can't turn your head off and yet can't come up with any answers. You're on a treadmill; but you don't know where you got on, and you don't know how to get off. You start to wonder where it is all going to end. *Am I losing my mind?* you ask yourself. *Maybe I am going crazy. No sane person would live this way.* And you just may be right.

Sex Problems

As communication in other areas of your marriage breaks down, the physical expression of closeness breaks down as well. You use sex as a weapon. You withhold sex if your husband doesn't behave himself. He can't have you in bed if he's going to drink like that. *Go to bed with your mistress or the bottle!* you think.

You may be repulsed by the smell of the liquor, which is reason enough to reject his overtures. You assume he wants you out of lust and not love anyway. You may, however, submit to him because you figure that if he is sexually satisfied he will go to sleep and leave you alone. You may also think in terms of your wifely role and responsibility. So you have the choice of feeling guilty or degraded. Once again your self-esteem has been reduced.

Sexual abuse is not uncommon. Women submit to behavior they would resist if they had any self-respect left. Clients tell me of actions resulting in the need for medical attention. It is hard for them even to tell me what happened. But these unfortunate women gather their courage to tell me so that I can give them permission not to allow it to happen again. I give my client permission to be a person. "I just couldn't live anymore without telling someone," Judy D. said to me. "And I know that you're not allowed to tell anybody." I don't have to be more specific. You know what I'm talking about. You know the difference between creative sex that is pleasurable, and abuse. In the sexual sphere, as in every other sphere in your life, you lose a sense of yourself as a worthy person and become afraid and confused.

It is not unusual for an alcoholic to have an affair. He complains, "My wife doesn't understand me." You sure as hell don't! "She doesn't want me in bed." Well, he's right. "She won't drink with me." You tried it, but you've developed an aversion to the stuff by this time. It doesn't matter that the affair is a symptom of the disease—you are shattered. Your identity is so tied up with him that you are beside yourself. *I'm obviously not much of a woman*, you conclude. *If I were, this affair would not have happened.* Your self-image thus takes another downward plunge. You're a bad wife, mother, housekeeper, and now—you've lost your sexuality. You're a nothing. Baloney! You're a victim. You're a casualty of near-alcoholism.

Some couples are able to maintain a satisfying sex life until the later stages of the disease, when the husband becomes impotent. The problem here is that you think that because you can be so loving in bed, everything else will be all right. This hope, too, is shattered. Your expectations get you into trouble. And you can only be disappointed. There can be no winning until you learn how to give up your false hopes and live in the moment. You will.

Anger

Anger, in one form or another, is always present in the alcoholic home. The tension is thick enough to cut with a knife. What will he say? What will he do? I'll kill him if he doesn't leave me alone. Will he damage the car? Will he wake up the kids? Should I ask him for the money? All these uncertainties lead to anger with people you are not really angry at. A simple request from your child turns you into a screaming shrew. "I only asked if I. . . . You didn't have to . . . ," the poor kid cries. Then when you realize what you've done, you are angry with yourself.

Quarreling is almost constant. The alcoholic quarrels in order to find an excuse to drink and the nonalcoholic quarrels because everything he says or does turns her off. It seems that no other kind of conversation is possible. "Pass the peas," he snarls, only to be answered with, "What, is your arm broken?"

You punish: "Fix your own dinner. I've had it!" You try to get even: "You won't see my folks. I won't see yours!" You threaten to leave. If you actually do, you find yourself out in the car in the middle of the night with no place to go. You become rigid and distrustful. Rage consumes you without a satisfying outlet. Anyone who walks into your house can feel the angry vibrations.

There is no escape from it. Who ever thought you would turn into such a self-righteous witch?

This tension, however, does not always show itself in your behavior. If you are living with violence, you may keep it inside rather than risk an assault. It's a difficult but realistic choice. If it is inner-directed, that is, if you continually keep your mouth shut even though you feel the need to explode, the tension will probably make you physically ill. Colitis, gastritis and ulcers are not uncommon in families of alcoholics. Anger that is not let out can literally eat your guts out. I am not advocating that you open up your mouth. The consequences may not be worth it. I will, in a later chapter, talk about productive ways to get rid of your anger.

Lethargy, Hopelessness, Self-Pity, Remorse, Despair

No matter what you do, no matter how hard you try, it isn't enough. You give and you give as if the well has no bottom. After a while you give up. What's the difference? Nothing you do will change anything. You are physically and mentally exhausted. You are tired of carrying the world on your shoulders. You just can't do it anymore. You reach a point where you lose interest in everything. Your emotional energy is drained, and you feel hopeless and alone. You are filled with self-pity and remorse. Getting through each day becomes a chore. Getting out of bed and getting dressed are overwhelming tasks. What's the use of going on? *It simply isn't worth it,* you think. Consequently, you give up. You withdraw into an isolated existence.

When you reach this point of despair, you yourself may start drinking or taking drugs. It's incredible, but the alcohol wins again. You don't care anymore, and you feel as if you can't face another day. Your problems are too great. Your life has become totally unmanageable. You want out.

Identify with any of this? Any of it have any special meaning to you? You betcha! I give you my word I haven't been in your house. But I've been in a hundred other houses, and I've talked to a hundred other women who have lived your life. You're not alone. It's a big and not very exclusive club.

I am reminded of the airline pilot who said to his passengers, "I have some bad news and some good news. The bad news is . . . we're lost. The good news is . . . we're making excellent time." It's amazing how much you expend going round and round in circles. You may not believe it now, but you have the power to say, "Hey, wait a minute. I want to get off." This book will show you how.

What Happens
to the Children

What about the children? They are the most vulnerable of all. They are victims and they are powerless. They are dependent and defenseless. They know no other way of life. You and your husband are the most important people in their world. You are the ones they turn to to know that they are loved, that they are worthy, and that no harm will come to them. What do they get? They get a lot of mixed messages. You say, "I love you—leave me alone." You say, "Don't worry," as the lines dig deep in your forehead. You feel their pain, but don't know how to take it away. It's hard for a child to know what is really being said. What happens goes something like this: You spend much of your time and energy reacting to your husband both when he is there and when he is not. So do your children. They also spend time and energy reacting to you. They react not only to you and to your reactions to their father, but to your actions and reactions toward them. Sound confusing? You bet. They cannot think clearly when their life is so muddled. Nothing makes a lot of sense. The only certainty is the uncertainty. The only consistency is the inconsistency.

So they become confused. If you live with confusion, you get confused. There is no alternative. The smoke does not clear. Children imitate their parents. This is one of the ways that they learn who they are. Somebody is always saying, "You have your mother's eyes," or,

"You're built just like your father." Kids don't say, "Hey, wait a minute! These are my eyes," or, "This is my body." We tend to look toward family to explain certain things we see in our children. My daughter has played the piano since she was five years old. My mother said, "She gets that from your brother." It may or may not be true, but it's a nice feeling. It's a nice feeling because they share something special. These comparisons are also made in destructive ways. "I wasn't surprised when Johnny Jones got busted for drugs. After all, his father's a drunken bum." This happens a lot. I bite my lip a lot, too, because I know that the son of this self-righteous person was Johnny Jones's connection. The point is that even in this age of individuality, adages like a chip off the old block, or the apple doesn't fall far from the tree, carry a degree of truth.

They carry truth not only because of what I've just said, but because that is the way that children learn. They learn through identification. As I write this book, my oldest son is working on a short story, my daughter a song, and my baby a God-knows-what. He can't read it back. They may be conscious or unconscious of what they are doing, but they pattern themselves anyway. We communicate to them what our values are and they pick them up as their own. If we are unclear, they will be unclear. They will role-play the adult. House is a favorite

game among children. Let's take a look at what your
children have to model their dolls after. It's not the
Brady Bunch.

The alcoholic father is inconsistent. He is thought of
mostly in terms of broken promises. When he is sober, he
makes commitments to the children. "I'd love to take you
to the game Saturday." "Sure, I'll buy you that toy."
When he says this, he really means it. But it rarely comes
about. The children never know what to believe. They
do not know from day to day, hour to hour, how he is
going to treat them. When he is sober, he acts like the
ideal parent. He tries especially hard because he feels
rotten about his behavior when he was drinking. He is
loving, affectionate, understanding, indulgent and
companionable. He is all the things a child would want.
He makes the child feel that everything will be okay. He
will make it so. The child takes this all in. He needs this
and it makes him feel good inside. Then when the
drunken episode occurs, and his father is mean and bru-
tal, he is shattered. His whole world falls apart. He
doesn't know what is real. He doesn't know what to
depend on or what to trust. He wants to believe in the
good father, but he can't. He can't stand the thought of
believing in the bad one. He bounces back and forth not
knowing that this isn't the way things have to be. After
all, this is what he knows. Since the idea of what a father

is is all mixed up, and since this is all the child knows, the son of an alcoholic father has trouble seeing himself as a more typical adult male. He simply doesn't know what it is. The horror is that alcoholism itself becomes part of the father role that the boy identifies with. As a result we find that a high percentage of alcoholics also come from homes where one or more parents abused alcohol.

On the surface, you would think that just the opposite would be true. You would think that the children would develop an aversion to alcohol. Some do, but more do not. Unless these children experience other alternatives, they will repeat the same mistakes. "I can hold my liquor. I'll never be a drunk like my father." Chances are his father said the same thing.

The daughter gets confused, too. She may think of a man who drinks as manly and independent. It doesn't make a lot of sense, but that's what happens. As a result, we find that daughters of alcoholics are more likely to marry active or potential alcoholics than daughters of nonalcoholics. Here again, they don't do it on purpose. They are not consciously aware of what they are doing. Many girls marry their "fathers." It is not unusual, but in this instance, it is unfortunate.

So much for the child's view of the alcoholic. Now let's take a look at how the children see you. They do not see you as terrific, either. You are in an impossible position.

You try to shield your children, but it doesn't work out the way you want. Your protection of the children leads to a lot of half-truths and white lies. After all, you don't want them to worry. You don't want their father's drinking to become *their* problem, if you can help it. Since children react to feelings as much as to words, they know something is not quite right. They know you are not being completely honest with them. They want to know and yet they don't want to know. If they ask, you snap at them, "Nothing is bothering me!" "If nothing is bothering you, why are you snapping at me? I didn't do anything." It goes downhill from there. Or they don't ask, but that doesn't mean they are not concerned. They are concerned because they know, and yet they don't know, what is going on. They know something is wrong but they don't know what. They really don't understand. And you can't make them understand because you don't really understand yourself, and besides, you'd rather not get into it. After all, what good would it do?

Even though, in your moments of anger, you have let the children know what a horror their father is, it is not unusual for them to be more angry with you than with him. After all, you are the one responsible for saying no to them. The discipline is not often shared. You are the one who is tired and irritable and takes it out on them. How can you possibly have the patience that children require when you have been up all the night before with a drunken husband who has followed you from room to room? I know one woman who was up night after night cleaning up the mess so the children wouldn't find it, indulging the alcoholic so he wouldn't be noisy and wake up the children, and waiting up until he was ready to pass out so that she could get him to bed and the children wouldn't find him passed out on the floor the next morning. She overheard her children talking about her. They said, "My mother's always so tired. I hardly ever see her anymore." They didn't know. Even if they did they would still feel the loss.

You are also the safest one to be angry at. They know what will happen if they are angry at you. They may not like it, but with their father anything can happen. So you get all of it. They cling to you, and yet hold you responsible. You weep for them, but wish they would leave you alone. Just a few minutes' peace. Isn't there an end to it?

The alcoholic home is not hard to identify. It goes something like this:

The air is fraught with tension. It is only a matter of time before the quarreling begins. It begins for reasons that don't make sense. The alcoholic will start an argument as an excuse to go out and drink. You will start an argument because of something that happened five days or five months or five years ago. The argument itself will be over some dumb thing that doesn't matter anyway. "What time is it?" "What, are you blind?"

Mary was telling me that her parents were arguing about what her curfew should be. She was furious because they wouldn't listen to her. She wanted to express her point of view, since it was her curfew. I explained to her that the argument was really not about her. It was a power play. The argument itself had to do not with Mary, but with her mother putting the drunk down where he belonged, and his fighting the bitch who was driving him to drink. Mary is the victim of the decision, but she is not relevant to the argument. After a while these arguments become just words to the child— angry words. Right or wrong doesn't matter because none of it makes any sense. The child responds with fear and soon learns that grown-ups don't always say what they mean or mean what they say.

Eventually, truth loses its meaning. In my own research with children from alcoholic homes, I found that they had lost a sense of truth. They didn't know what was true and what was not true. It also wasn't very important to them. They would guess at what they were supposed to feel. I gave a questionnaire to 150 children. One hundred of these children came from alcoholic homes. The fifty that did not were the same as the others in terms of age, sex and background. The only difference was that they did not have a parent who abused alcohol. Within this questionnaire is a lie scale. It is a way of finding out if someone is giving you the answers they think you want, rather than telling the truth. They do this in order to get a high score. The results showed that the children from nonalcoholic homes who lied, lied for just that reason. The children from alcoholic homes had much higher lie scores. These results showed that they were not lying. Their scores came out low whether they lied or not. This result pointed to the fact that their world is not a typical world. Therefore, their answers are not typical answers.

Beyond that, to complicate the issue still further, behaviors and attitudes that one would consider strange in a more typical home situation can be even healthy in the alcoholic home situation.

I had a twelve-year-old boy referred to me about a year ago. George had been disruptive in school. All the stories he wrote and drawings he made had to do with death and murder. There was lots of blood and violence and stabbing and shooting. He was doing poor school work as well. Both his parents and the school were concerned. He went to a summer program for special help and was then sent to me for emotional problems.

He came willingly. It has been my experience that children from alcoholic homes are very anxious to be able to talk to someone that they can trust. Keeping it all inside is almost too much to bear. As he spoke, he told me of a dream he had. The dream involved man-eating ants attacking his home. He, because of his bravery, was able to lead his mother and grandmother to safety. For some reason his father remained stuck in the house and when they returned, all that was left of him was a part of an intestine. Interesting dream? Yes. Interesting in a lot of ways. Sound like a kid in trouble? Yes. No question of that. But the dream itself is not a sign of mental illness.

This boy was living in a home where his father was an active alcoholic. His life was a living hell. He could not show his anger to his father. He was afraid of him. His mother chose to avoid the issue and became overprotective of the boy.

No wonder the boy was screaming "KILL!" He was very angry. Who wouldn't be? If he had not shown any outward signs of his anger, he would have been far more disturbed.

I saw the boy for a short period of time, and then I began to see his mother. If the climate in the home could be changed, the boy would react differently. If I could get her healthy, the boy could be healthy. And that's just about the way it went. The mother's changed attitudes allowed the boy to grow and to talk about his feelings.

He was able to find ways of behaving that were more acceptable. The dreams stopped and so did the drawings. I saw him last week. His father is no longer drinking and they are all working hard at being a family. He smiles now. He no longer hates the world. He's doing better in school. He's in less trouble. Now when he fails a test, or gets into a fight, it's because he didn't study or because boys get into fights. It's not because he couldn't concentrate while worrying about his mother worrying about his father, or because he wanted to beat up the world.

In this case, the child cried out for help and it was recognized. Other children withdraw and are left alone because they are no trouble. Others end up in jail. "Who cares what I do!" Others are referred to child guidance clinics. The prognosis for mental health is very poor without help. And with your help we can perform miracles. The results are almost immediate. But before you can help, it is important to look at the full picture.

It does not get less complicated, but it all falls into place so that you can understand what is happening. As you read further you may start to feel depressed and guilty. Don't be discouraged. These children can be helped. Just between you and me, that's why I love working with families of alcoholics. I have success. I will give you the tools and you will have success too.

As our environment acts on us in negative ways, it can

act on us in positive ways. These children have very few consistent, supportive experiences in their lives. As a result, their self-esteem is badly damaged. It has to be. The way that we learn to think that we are worth something depends on a number of things. A person's self-esteem has to do with the degree to which he thinks he is capable, significant, successful and worthy. Much of this is determined by the way he is treated by others. He takes on the ideas and attitudes of the important people in his life as his own.

The child from the alcoholic home does not see himself as capable. If he was truly capable, he would be able to figure out a way to get his father to stop drinking. Everything else pales by comparison. He dismisses anything that he does as unimportant. What difference does it make if he can build something, or can get A's in math, if his father is drunk all the time and his mother is preoccupied and nobody really cares?

I was shown a self-portrait made by a very bright fourth-grade boy who lived with a violent, abusive alcoholic father. Under the drawing the child had written, "I wish I was dead. I'm so stupid." His self-image was far from his capabilities. He was behaving according to his self-image.

He had been placed with an insensitive teacher who did not understand his pleas for help. We were able to

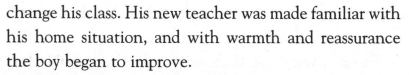

change his class. His new teacher was made familiar with his home situation, and with warmth and reassurance the boy began to improve.

Significant? To whom? His father is more concerned with his next drunk. His mother is thinking up ways to try to prevent that. How can he be significant? He gets in the way. And he feels in the way.

I was asked by a family to interview their sixteen-year-old son, who was being held in a youth detention center. It was their hope that if I wrote a favorable report, it could be used in the boy's defense when he came to trial.

Ned had been involved with a very serious crime and the whole community was outraged. As we sat and talked, I said to him, "I don't understand what made you do it. I've known you a long time and it just doesn't sound like your style." He said, "I did it so they'd notice me."

Does that send chills up your spine? It did mine. His family had been so consumed with his father's drinking that they really had paid no attention. He had gotten expelled from school. They paid no attention. He was involved in petty crimes, each time leaving evidence for his parents to find. Nothing. And finally he did something that got their attention. It got a lot of people's attention. And, it cost a boy a year in jail. For him, for children who act out in order to be noticed, the nature of the attention is not nearly as important as the attention itself. *At least they know I'm alive. Let them worry about me for a change.*

They feel worthless because they feel responsible for their father's illness. If they were better kids, their father would not drink. And, of course, there is no way that they can be good enough. So these feelings are continually reinforced.

What happens in terms of their attitudes toward home is interesting. You would assume that the kids would want to run away. You would assume that they would want to get just as far away from that situation as they possibly could. This is not true. These kids have very mixed feelings. Although they are unhappy at home, they feel needed. How can their mother manage without them? They worry about their father. Although they are angry with the alcoholic, or the irritable nonalcoholic, they feel somehow responsible. They hunger for the love of the rejecting parent, and this binds them up emotionally. This has an effect on their self-concept. They feel guilty. They can't let go of the feeling that it is something wrong with them that caused their parent to drink. There must be something they can do to get their father to stop drinking. These attitudes are supported by the alcoholic who does not want to take responsibility for his behavior. This is also an attitude that they picked up from you because you are thinking the same things for

yourself. It gets complicated. The children want to protect their mother. They want to be protected by their
mother. Their father isn't *always* horrible. Maybe he'll
stop as he promised. Their emotions are greatly tied up
in their home. Even when they leave the home, they
have not left emotionally. The college students that I
have, who come from alcoholic homes, are far more concerned with what is happening at home than those students from more typical homes. The phone calls are
traumatic. They need me. I owe them. Can they get
along without me? It is a different feeling than I get from
the other students. From them I get comments such as,
"My folks are trying to lay a guilt trip on me because I
don't call or come home as often as they want me to."
They may feel guilty, but it doesn't appear, in general, to
be as wrenching. It is the struggle to grow up and be
independent, even if it means being selfish and thought-
less. Although, as a parent, none of us like that stage
because it feels like a kick in the teeth, it is healthier
than the constant checking up and running home to be
sure that everything is still there.

Social relationships must of necessity suffer. The children are afraid to establish friendships because they are
embarrassed to invite their friends home. They don't
know what will happen, or how their friends will be
treated when they arrive. And they have cause to be con-

cerned. Since they cannot explain ahead of time, and since eventually invitations from others must be returned, they are embarrassed. I know of one little girl who brought a friend home with her from school and found her father passed out on the living room floor. Her mother told the friend that he had a bad back and the doctor had told him that sleeping on the floor would be good for it. The girl seemed to believe it at the time, but she never returned.

What happens to these kids is that they withdraw so that they do not have to face others, or they act out in such a manner that others will reject them. It is just too painful to deal with. This adds to the feeling of aloneness and lack of worth. "Everybody hates me. I have no friends. No matter what I do I get into trouble."

School performance and attitudes suffer as well. It is hard to imagine how one can concentrate on schoolwork when he is worried about what is going on at home, or has been kept up most of the night by an alcoholic parent. Attention span is something that is learned and developed. Under these circumstances, it is almost impossible.

A teacher who is sensitive to the needs of children—who establishes an accepting, caring climate—can provide a haven for these children. I think this is shown by the following essay written by a seventh-grade girl from an alcoholic home. Although she doesn't state it, she is reflecting back on a time when her father was actively drinking.

Dreams

I seldom remember my dreams. I think dreams are just things you think about while you are asleep. I am pretty sure that I am accurate. I once had a dream that a huge monster came to town. He killed everyone in sight, and smashed up houses with people in them. I would see him before anyone did, it always turned out that no one else noticed that he was there except for me. I would run to the Seniors' house two houses away, and hide on their new porch. They had just added a porch in real life when I had the dream. Anyway I would hear screams and really get scared. I started to cry, when all of a sudden, the monster picks me up and starts talking to me. I was really scared then, I was sure he'd trample me. But he didn't. I'm sure he would have if I wasn't crying. He became very sentimental, and was very nice to me. It turned out that I was all alone because the monster had killed everyone in the world except for me. The monster kept me company, then one day I turned and he was gone, I was all alone again, but this time it was for good.

What that dream seems to mean is that I was angry and I wanted to get back at people who had hurt me in any way. So I was really the monster getting back at those people by killing them. Then, after I had killed them I was all alone, which is where I started from. When I had that dream I was in third grade. I had no friends at home, because I was shy and very sensitive. Whenever someone did something mean to me, I'd really get upset. I hated a lot of people. I was a real mess. Probably the reason I liked school was because it was a way to get away from problems around home. In school I was the comedian, and had a lot of friends. I tried to be funny to hide my real feelings.

It is hard for the teachers to identify these children as sufferers of near-alcoholism. They don't want it known. I have asked kids, of varying ages, if they would join a group in school to help them live with this problem, if their names were kept confidential. Each has said, "Forget it! I won't take the risk of someone finding out!" I am starting such a group at the college where I teach. I find that out of every ten students I see, at least two are somehow touched by this problem. Astounding figures, but true. I don't know how many will join the group. The admission to others is devastating, but the response of "I know exactly what you're talking about because it happened to me, too," brings with it such enormous relief, you can almost observe a great weight being lifted. They stand taller.

Although the picture I've painted may look pretty grim, it is far from hopeless. Just as soon as you begin to get better, your children will get better. It is practically automatic. You can recover as a family. The very illness that has divided the family can bring it together. I have seen it work so often.

Alcoholism is a family disease. Part of its strategy is to divide and conquer. It gains strength when each member of the family retreats into his own private hell. But when the family joins as a unit to combat it, it loses its power to control and dominate. It becomes neutralized. It loses the sick energy that it needs to feed on. The struggle it puts up is enormous, but once the family is not afraid, it can only feed on itself. Eventually it loses its power, and you gain yours back.

This book will give you the tools to work with. It will give you a way to help yourself and then, more specifically, it will give you the tools that will help the children.

As I said earlier, children learn through identification and role modeling. They give back what is given to them. As you change, you present to them a person that they can feel good about. You become a person they want to be like. As you are better able to share your thoughts and feelings, so will they. As you learn to accept yourself, so will they be better able to accept themselves. When you learn to love yourself, they will learn to love themselves. And finally, you will learn to make your energy work for you and not against you. It's not easy—but it's worth it.

Coming to Grips
with the Problem

The first step in making your life manageable is to accept alcoholism as a disease. It is a disease as diabetes is a disease, or cancer is a disease. It is a progressive disease. It gets worse by stages. It is a fatal disease. It can be arrested, but it cannot be cured.

Nobody can really pinpoint what happens in the body of an alcoholic when he takes a drink. Something happens that is not the same as when a nonalcoholic takes a drink. The alcohol does not follow the same digestive process that it does in a nonalcoholic. I recently heard an alcoholic say, "I took a swallow and felt it in my toes." "I tried a taste of chocolate mousse that I didn't know had brandy in it, and I started to tingle." The sensitivity to the drug is immediately apparent.

I know of an alcoholic man who had not had a drink in eight years. He started working in a paint factory. The alcohol in the paint fumes triggered off his addiction, and he went on a bender.

I have an alcoholic student who bounces off the walls when she takes antihistamine for a cold. Her body reacts the same way to all drugs.

I know of many recovering alcoholics who will not use aspirin for a headache, refuse Novocaine at the dentist, watch the mouthwash labels, and take other extreme precautions because they are terrified that the slightest ingestion of any drug into their system will cause them to lose control. The fact of the matter is that there is a good chance that they are right.

Alcohol addicts its victims both psychologically and physically. Usually the psychological addiction is the most apparent in the early stages. In R. D. Laing's book *Knots*, he describes the pattern of psychological addiction. Although there may be variations on the theme, I find what he says to be pretty much the way it is. (I have changed she to he.)

> He has started to drink
>> as a way to cope
>> that makes him less able to cope
>
> the more he drinks
> the more frightened he is of
>> becoming a drunkard
>> the more drunk
> the less frightened of being drunk
>
> the more frightened of being drunk
>> when not drunk
>> the more not frightened drunk
>> the more frightened not drunk

Round and round we go. I think you get the picture. The victim gets sucked in deeper and deeper. The image that comes to mind is that of quicksand, but I've been told you can float on top of quicksand. There's no floating with alcoholism. Things may appear to stabilize, but that's a part of the deception.

As the psychological addiction progresses, so does the physical. Consider this. Alcohol is made up of both ethyl and methyl alcohol. The ethyl alcohol is what makes us feel good, and is absorbed quickly into the system. Methyl alcohol is similar to embalming fluid. This takes longer to break down. Because of its nature, it is the methyl alcohol that is responsible for the morning-after hangover. I'm sure you've been told that the best remedy for a hangover is a drink. This is so because it slows down the methyl alcohol and the ethyl alcohol is absorbed. You feel better for a time. Then, if you continue to choose to avoid the pain, you just have another drink. This slows down the process of the methyl alcohol and the ethyl alcohol is absorbed and you feel better for a time—and then if you want to avoid the pain you just have another drink and this slows down the process of the methyl alcohol and the ethyl alcohol. . . . Many alcoholics don't have hangovers because the level of alcohol in their bloodstream never gets low enough for the methyl alcohol to start to break down.

What I have talked about so far are the early stages. The disease gets progressively worse. As it takes greater hold, there is the physical compulsion. Many develop physical symptoms, such as the shakes, which are calmed by alcohol. Others hallucinate. Alcohol causes the devils, and then offers itself as the only thing the alcoholic can use to drive them away.

Many alcoholics die from damage to body organs, such as the liver or the pancreas. Alcohol takes such a strong hold on the sick alcoholic that he can even risk death when he tries to withdraw. Cold-turkey withdrawal from alcohol can be dangerous. One does not die from cold-turkey withdrawal from heroin, but one can with alcohol. Detoxification centers watch alcoholics very carefully when they are going through withdrawal. Rehabilitation centers, in general, will not accept an alcoholic until he has been detoxified. The risks of convulsion are too great for nonmedical people to handle. I cannot believe that a person who was not insane would poison himself to this degree. This is not an act of moral weakness. This is a sickness.

If you believe nothing else that I have told you in this book, believe that alcoholism is a disease. I know it is difficult to accept, but the evidence is overwhelming. I have spoken to so many women who just cannot believe it. No matter what I say, and no matter how much they trust me, they still can't stop thinking, "If he *really* wanted to, he could quit!" Interestingly enough, while these women cannot accept the disease concept for their husbands, they are scared to death that their children will inherit it.

One thing that may get in the way of your accepting alcoholism as a disease, is the stereotype of the Skid Row bum—out of work, no family, cruddy clothes, grubby beard, brown bag hiding a bottle, wiping windshields of cars for change to buy more rot gut.

The stereotype is true—for a few. I admit I used to believe it myself, but then I got to know some alcoholics. Some were out of work. Some were working. There were unskilled laborers and high corporate executives, doctors, lawyers, you name it. Incomes ranged from being on welfare to $200,000 a year. Some were Irish Catholics, some Protestants, some Jews, white, black, old, young, brilliant, slow. The only statement that can be made for all these people is that *they all have a problem with alcohol*.

The stereotype is not the only myth that gets in the way of your accepting the disease. There are a number of others. "He never drinks during the day," "He doesn't drink all that much," "He only drinks on the weekend," or, "He never drinks on the weekend." The fact remains that it doesn't matter when he drinks, how much he drinks, or what time of the day he begins. What matters is whether he loses control once he takes the first drink. As the disease progresses, he will drink earlier and earlier. The fact that he delays the first one, does not mean he is not alcoholic.

"He only drinks beer." A bottle of beer has the same amount of alcohol as a shot of whiskey. A six-pack of beer is like three double shots. You get more bloat, but you don't get less alcohol.

"He's too young to be an alcoholic." Alcoholism is not

a function of age. As a matter of fact, the disease progresses faster in a young person than in an older one. I
recently heard a man in his early twenties proclaim that
he didn't start drinking seriously until he was eight.
Incredible? Believe it.

Attend an open meeting of Alcoholics Anonymous.
You'll see the same assortment of people that you see at
a PTA meeting, or a church group, or on the beach.
Some of them will be the identical people. You will hear
them talk about the things they did when they were
drinking, because they are afraid that if they don't "keep
their memories green" they will repeat them.

At the first AA meeting that I attended, I heard an
elderly woman speak. She talked about attending a wake
many years ago. At that time they still packed bodies in
ice, and she hid some beer bottles under the ice in the
casket. Now she knew how alcoholic that thinking was.
Alcoholism, if left unchecked, will drive you insane—if
it does not kill you first.

Who is an alcoholic? It comes down to this: An alcoholic is anybody who is suffering from the disease of
alcoholism. That's it. I know that sounds much too
simple, but the understanding and acceptance of that
statement are the beginning steps toward *your* recovery.

I mention once again how important it is to realize
that alcoholism is a disease. The alcoholic is a sick per-

son. He does not choose to behave the way he does. It is the chemical within his system that dictates his behavior. It is not his choice. Ingesting the chemical is not his choice. It is not a sign of moral weakness. He has a compulsion over which he has no control. No one chooses to be an alcoholic. Someone may choose to take a drink. If that someone is not alcoholic, he still has a choice after the first one as to whether or not he will have a second. The alcoholic does not have such a choice. After the first drink, the compulsion sets in, and even though he may be able to control his drinking for certain periods of time, the compulsion will eventually take over and he will drink until he can drink no more.

The other key word in that sentence is suffering. The alcoholic is not a happy person. Alcohol is a depressant. So regardless of the real or imagined reasons he uses in order to justify his drinking, he is miserable much of the time, if only because of the effect of the chemical. The initial feeling of freedom that allows him to be the life of the party gives way to depression. It is an emotional depression if he is embarrassed by his behavior, and a chemical depression because of the nature of the drug.

There are many definitions of alcoholism. None of them is entirely satisfactory. It is not really necessary for us to know them all. We all know what an alcohol abuser looks like. We can all make some assumptions about what an alcohol abuser behaves like. And we all know, when the subject of alcohol abuse comes up, what we are talking about.

For our purposes, an alcoholic is best defined as someone whose drinking causes a continuing and growing problem in any area of his life—more specifically, someone whose drinking is causing a continuing and growing problem in *your* life. It may be seen as a problem by you long before it is seen as a problem by him. And furthermore, what really truly matters is not whether your husband is an alcoholic by whatever definition, but your reaction to his drinking. Nancy H. called me the other day. She said, "Maybe it's me. Maybe he's not an alcoholic. He says he isn't, but I treat him as if he is!"

I say to you what I said to Nancy. It doesn't matter whether or not your husband is an alcoholic. You are reacting to him as if he is and, therefore, you have to work on yourself.

And so we begin.

The first thing to do is to begin to work on changing your attitude. If your husband were dying of cancer and his disease was causing him to be obnoxious, the obnoxious behavior would make you upset and angry, but you would not hold him responsible for his cancer. The same thing holds true with alcoholism. You cannot hold an alcoholic responsible for his alcoholism. You can hold him responsible for his behavior. Chances are you have done the reverse. You have thought of him as a bastard when he drank himself blotto, and then found a way to blame yourself for his ranting and raving. In so doing, you have enabled the disease.

What a harsh thing for me to say to you—harsh, but true. You have probably been an unwilling accomplice to alcoholism. You have, for all the right reasons, done all the wrong things. You have probably covered up for him, blamed him and not the disease, made aimless threats, joined him in drinking, become extremely emotional, used self-pity and self-deception, tried to control his drinking, and taken over his responsibilities.

All of those responses are understandable. All of those responses are perfectly normal. All of those responses help to make his continued drinking possible. It may not make sense to you yet, but it should as we go on. Even when you see how these responses enable the disease, you may not choose, for your own survival, to eliminate all of them. But you will be aware, and being aware will open up new options for you.

There are two physical responses to alcohol that are helpful for you to understand, before you can stop enabling his alcoholism and feel good about it. The first has to do with the anesthetic nature of the drug, and the second response is blackouts.

Alcohol is an anesthetic. Before the development of more

sophisticated anesthetics, it was used for this purpose. It insulates one physically and emotionally against pain. The pain that you or I feel when someone is hurtful to us, goes unfelt by the alcoholic who is drinking. What that means is that anything that we do that lessens the consequences of his drinking helps him to continue drinking. He has to be hurt so badly that he can feel the hurt through the drug. He has to hurt so badly that he will cry for help. You don't know what it is that will make him hurt badly enough, but the enabling stops the pain and delays the moment of truth.

Alcoholics are also prone to blackouts. A blackout is a period of time when an individual functions in a seemingly normal manner, but has no memory of it. He only knows he has been in one when he comes out of it, and he doesn't have any sense of how he got where he is. A blackout is a very frightening experience. I have heard some of the most incredible stories of what has gone on during blackouts. One man told me of being transferred by his company from Newark to Boston. He was happy about the transfer and went out to celebrate. When he came out of the blackout, he found that he had enlisted in the Canadian army. That blackout cost that man five years.

Many a businessman will make a series of phone calls while in a blackout. Then, the next day, remake those same calls. Not too good for business. But he had no recollection of having done it before.

I know a man who claims his last child was conceived in a blackout. His wife called it rape, and his friends have a great time teasing him that he can never be completely sure that it is his child.

Blackouts are strong evidence of alcoholism. Non-alcoholics will pass out before they black out, or they will stop drinking when they have had enough.

I bring up these two examples of the effects of alcohol to help you understand the importance of changing your behavior. Many of us who work in this field maintain that an alcoholic will not seek help until he has hit his "bottom." He will only hit his bottom when the repercussions of his behavior are too overwhelming for him to ignore. Keep in mind that any behavior of yours that allows the alcoholic to avoid the consequences of his actions, lengthens the life of the disease. Any behavior of yours that causes the alcoholic to take responsibility for his behavior, *may* help shorten it. We don't know for sure what will make a difference, but we know the direction. Since we are dealing with such an insidious disease, the opposite of the usual rules apply. You will behave in ways that are contrary to your nature if you are a loving, supportive, caring, nurturing person. The way you demonstrate your love is by letting your alcoholic endure his own suffering. If you cushion that for him because you love him, and want to make him feel better because you are a good person, *you are helping to kill him*. I recognize that this is a very strong statement. I don't know how to make it any stronger. I would if I could.

I know of one man who had to go away on a business trip in order to crash to his bottom and seek help. Somehow his wife, no matter how hard she tried not to, found a way to patch up his wounds, and his disease continued to progress. When he finally got away and there was no one to apply the emotional bandages, he had a psychotic break—technical term for "he lost his mind"—and was finally able to get help. His wife, recognizing this was beyond her scope, had him hospitalized. Since he was crazy as a result of the alcohol, his hallucinations ceased after a few days and his paranoid delusions stopped. He then went to a rehabilitation center to begin his recovery. The point here is that his wife, with the best of intentions, was only doing harm.

There are many ways that you enable the disease. Most of them are ways in which you thought you were being helpful. You may also have been afraid to act differently. It may be that the risks of behaving differently are too great for you. You must be prepared to handle the outcome of your behavior. As I discuss enabling or rescuing behaviors, be aware of this behavior in yourself. Then look at it, and see if it is truly in your best interest to continue. You know that it is not in the best interest

of your husband *regardless of what he says*. He will try to
tell you otherwise. When trying to convince you, he will
try to lay guilt on you and may threaten you. At that
point, if you stand your ground, he will either back off or
attack. More often than not, the surprise at your asser-
tion will cause him to back off, but, as I've said many
times, the behavior is unpredictable and you have to be
prepared for whatever happens. The preparation is part
of the learning, but for now, let's just look at the
enabling behaviors. Let's look at what it is that you do
that enables him to avoid taking responsibility for his
actions and, thereby, facing their consequences.

The first of these is covering up for him. How many
times have you called his boss and told him that your
husband was not feeling well when he was hungover?
He's big enough to make that call for himself. How many
phone calls have come in when you have said that he
was out because he was too drunk to come to the phone?
Why not hand him the phone, and let him find a way to
struggle through the call?

Sheila's husband went out to play poker. She stayed up
most of the night worrying. When he ambled in at about
four in the morning, he had blood on his forehead. Her
fears were realized. He had been in an accident. A taxi
had had the misfortune to stop at a red light and Rob
had driven right into it. There was minor damage to the

cab, Rob's windshield was smashed, and his forehead was cut. Sheila was so relieved that he was not seriously hurt that any thought of herself went out the window. Do you start to smell the setup? "Sheila, dear, do you think you could take care of having the car repaired?" "Of course, honey; all that matters is that you're not hurt."

So, Sheila told the men at the body shop that it was her fault. She did all the paper work for the insurance company. She suffered all the aggravations one suffers when a car is repaired. Bob gets off free. His wife has covered for him and taken over his responsibility. He has not had to feel any consequences. He has paid no emotional price for drunken driving. Is that fair to him? The disease is the only beneficiary because Rob has lost out on an opportunity to feel the results of uncontrolled drinking. He must experience it if he is to get well. Sheila's loving act was, in reality, very cruel.

Another way that you may cover up is in not letting him find the fruits of his drunken labor. If he has smashed up the furniture the night before, or broken some dishes, it is important that when he awakens he sees them. There are a couple of reasons for this. The first has to do with you and your self-respect. Why should you clean up after him? Are you a servant in your own home? The second reason is that since alcoholics are prone to blackouts, there is a very real possibility that he simply will not remember. He would prefer to forget the whole thing, as if it never happened. Your cleaning it up will help him to do that. Telling him about it will not have the same impact, and may open up a whole other can of worms. The same applies to helping him to bed. Let him find himself on the floor when he awakens. That way, he will know that he really did pass out on the floor. Otherwise, you cannot be sure that he will believe it. It is a very painful memory. Alcoholics would prefer to avoid unpleasant memories.

You are naturally concerned about the children. You don't want the children to awaken and find the mess. You want to protect them from the harsh reality. Perfectly understandable. It just doesn't work. First of all, you make the assumption that the children slept through the whole thing. That is highly unlikely. Secondly, you are making the assumption that knowing something is wrong, and not knowing what it is, is better than knowing the truth. Rethink that. They know that something is wrong because they are not as sophisticated as adults. They feel it. They pick up what you are feeling and it is unsettling to them. If you want your kids to grow up strong and emotionally healthy, they *must* confront reality. Life is not always pleasant. You know for yourself that you can handle the truth more easily than a well-meaning lie. Children are not different in this regard.

What you do is simply tell them the truth *without anger*. "This is what happened last night when Daddy was drunk. I feel very sad that you have to see it, but I am not going to pick it up and I don't want you to either."

Let your husband see the mess. Let your husband clean up the mess. Let your husband be embarrassed for the children. He has a right to his humiliation. He earned it.

When you blame him and not his disease, you play into it. You act in accusatory ways that give him an excuse to get drunk. He feels guilty and resentful. He can hold you responsible. And he goes off to drink. If you accept the fact that he has a disease, you can blame the disease and not him. You can have compassion for him. Then you separate him from his illness. When he smashes up the furniture, you know that this is not the person you love smashing it up, but the disease. The person who wakes up the next morning, and is horrified at what his disease caused him to do, is the one you care about. All those angry feelings are gone, and he cannot even believe himself that he could have done that. If you tell him about it, he may need to think that you are exaggerating. And well you might be. He will also respond to your tone.

When you truly separate the person from the disease, and detach yourself from that part of it, you will send out different vibrations. Alcoholics are very sensitive people. They wait for a reaction from you. If you feel hostile, even if your words are kind, they feel the hostility and use it as an excuse to drink. Remember, they are like children in this regard. If you are truly compassionate and they do not feel tension coming from you, they have no excuse. This does not mean he will stay home and remain sober, but what it does mean is that he cannot use you as an excuse for his drinking. He has to admit, if only a little, that he is doing it for his own reasons, and not because of something that you have said or that you have done.

Remember Beth? It is entirely possible that Beth would not have required twenty-six stitches in her arm if she had been detached. This detachment that I speak of—and it is hard work—can save you a lot of grief. I don't know what words she said to her husband when he came upstairs and awakened her, but I do know that she was angry. He picked up on her tone and acted against it. If she had had compassion for his illness, even though she may have refused to leave her bed, her vibrations would not have said *kill*; they would have shown sympathy. He would not then have had anger to react to. This may not seem realistic to you yet, but keep reading. The pieces will fall into place.

Any behavior that allows him to use you as an excuse for drinking enables his disease. Crying, berating, inducing guilt—all give him an excuse to drink. He promises he'll stop and controls it for a while, but he can't, and your attitude plays into his need for a drink.

Hiding his bottles and pouring them down the sink only add to the expense. He'll learn to hide them better. *"She's not gonna decide if I can have liquor in my own house!"*

If you truly want him to get well, it is important that you do *nothing* to get in the way of his drinking. Read this again. I said what you think I said. If you really care about him, you will not find ways to get him to drink less. Any action of yours that causes him to control his drinking prolongs the life of the illness. Alcoholics, with few exceptions, need to get very sick before they get well. The faster they get very sick, the greater the chances of their recovery. So do not hide his bottles or extract "good behavior" promises. He has to stop by and for himself. He has to reach the point when the pain of drinking is greater than the pain of not drinking. Only he can know when that point is.

Your own ability to stay in touch with reality is essential. When you make excuses for his behavior, you don't help him know the situation for what it really is. You help him deny his addiction. He doesn't want to believe it, and if he cons you into thinking, "Things will work out all right," or, "I can control it," he can also con himself.

Drinking with him is a way of saying that his behavior is acceptable. If you can't lick 'em join 'em is a questionable hypothesis at best. You know that you're really only doing it to keep an eye on him. Maybe if you're with him, he won't drink as much.

More and more, you take over his responsibilities. You take over the checkbook. You mow the lawn. You do all the things you no longer trust him to do. This frees him to drink. This also means he doesn't have to answer to the bank. It also means he doesn't have to look at the overgrown grass. It may be that for yourself, you cannot leave these things unattended, and that's okay. Just be aware that it is a rescuing behavior. Be very sure you take over these responsibilities because you feel you must, for your own good and the good of your family. Martyrs are not appreciated during their lifetimes.

I realize that while you are reading this section, you are saying a lot of "yeah buts." I've heard them all. No, your situation is *not* different. No, your husband is *not* worse. No, you're no more afraid than anyone else in the same situation.

You're afraid you can't live with him.

You're afraid you can't live without him.

You're afraid he'll lose his job.

You're afraid he'll get killed.

You're afraid he'll kill you.

You're afraid of being alone.

You're afraid of a hundred things you can't even name.

What if . . . what if . . . what if . . .

That spinning feeling is not yours alone. And, you don't have to be lonely. There is help. There is Al-Anon. Al-Anon is a self-help group for families and friends of alcoholics. When you can muster up the courage, give them a call. You won't be asked to tell them anything you don't want them to know. They won't even ask you your name. They will just be happy that you've reached out for help. You will feel at home. You will tell these women (and men) of the horrors only you are living with, and they'll finish your sentences. They've been there. You'll hear someone talk and you'll think, *My God, they're talking about me!* You will feel a tremendous burden lifted. Once again, you have friends. The difference is that you have no secrets from these friends. They've lived your life because they're married to men like your husband. They know how you feel. At first, there will be one big difference between you and them. They'll know you're new to the group because of the pain on your face and your nearness to tears. You'll know who is not new because their eyes will be bright, and they can laugh. You'll get there, too, and the next chapter will start you off.

How You Can
Be Helped

This is the hard part. Concentrating on yourself is new to you. You have not been the center of your own universe. You have been spinning in your husband's orbit. You have been revolving around him.

You have been reacting to him. His reactions to you have been his reactions to your reactions to him. You have not been your own person. You have, in effect, become a nonperson.

This is not at all surprising. Even with the advent of the women's movement, many women still choose to live in the shadow of their husbands. For many women it is a satisfying way of life. In your situation, it is unhealthy. It will destroy you. In our society, it is not unusual for a woman to define herself in terms of her man and her children. You are so-and-so's wife and so-and-so's mother. Your husband's success is your success. The notion of the woman behind the man is still with us. His approval of you is your approval of you.

Your day is focused around his comings and goings. Pleasing him is all important. Since pleasing him is the most important thing in your life, you do not want to displease him. Since pleasing him becomes more and more difficult as he gets sicker and sicker, you try harder and harder. As a result you too get sicker and sicker. You gradually lose your sense of worth. You have not determined for yourself what your worth is, so when you are continually put down by your husband, you lose a sense of yourself. It doesn't happen overnight. The erosion process is so gradual as to go unnoticed. You have unwillingly allowed the disease of alcoholism to decide your value as a human being.

Now that you are becoming aware, let us begin to put all that in the past. It will not be easy. Start with today. You will begin to live in the present, one day at a time. This moment, right now, belongs to you. Grab on to it and make the most of it. Do it for yourself.

You will be faced with a new question. This question sounds very simple, but you will find it most difficult. You may not even understand it at first. The question is, "What do *I* want?" It is hard because you don't know for sure who "I" is. How long can you talk about yourself without mentioning another person? How many sentences can you write that start with the word I? How much of a conversation can you carry on talking about only your own thoughts and feelings? Take a look at how much of your conversation revolves around your husband and children. I'm not saying that is right or wrong. What I am saying is, can you make a conscious choice to talk only about yourself and be able to do it?

Linda discovered that she was pregnant. At first, she refused to believe it. But, as you and I both know, there are certain things that cannot be denied. Her marriage was a mess. Chuck's drinking was getting worse, and he continued to be violent. Linda's obstetrician had told her that she was not strong enough to carry to term. Her older children were frightened because she had miscarried before and it was very upsetting to them. Her mother had said, "What do you want to have a baby for?" The other women where she worked had said, "Your other kids are launched. You're starting a career. A baby will tie you down." There seemed to be a consensus that having a baby would not be a good idea.

Finally, someone said, "Linda, what do *you* want?" She was dumbfounded. What a strange question. That was the one question she had not considered. "What do I want?" She felt turned inside out. "What do I want?"

She gave it careful thought. She was seven months along and still thinking. Decisions are rough. It finally came to her. "I want to have a baby! After all, I'm the one who will have to live with whatever decision I make. I'm also the one who will have to take care of the baby once it is born." She finally knew that having the baby was the right decision for her.

I was with her when she delivered. I had never heard a mother laugh all through the labor and delivery. She had natural childbirth. It was only fitting. She was awake for the first time in a long time.

The baby is four now and he's wonderful. All the

people who advised her against it, love him dearly. She did what was right for *her* and everyone else benefited. They reacted to her joy and her positive attitude. Good feelings can be just as contagious as tension and anxiety. The bonus is that her husband is now sober and is a good father to the boy. But that's only a bonus. She had the baby because it was right for her and that's the best reason to do anything. She was able to answer the question, "What do I want?" Now it's your turn.

Let's take a look at some of the symptoms of near-alcoholism that we went over in the second chapter. Those things that drove you to despair can be examined in a new light. You can use your energy to work either for you or against you, now that you know you have the choice. Isn't that a powerful place to be? A person has choices. A person has options. You are a person. You will now become aware of what some of those options may be.

Denial

Isn't it about time you faced up to what's really happening? Cinderella is only a fairy tale. Your Prince Charming will probably puke in your glass slipper. The energy that you use to deny the truth can be put into facing it and not being victimized by it.

If you accept the fact that he will probably come home

Janet G. Woititz   101

drunk, you are prepared if he does, and pleasantly surprised if he does not. If you deny the probable, even
though he swore to you that he would never drink again,
you will be shattered if he disappoints you. You have, in
effect, set yourself up. It is unfair to blame him.

Reality may be rough, but it's the only way to keep
sane. I'm not suggesting that you give up hope. I'm just
suggesting you give up fantasy. "If only"—these two
words can lead to nothing but trouble. Some people live
out their whole lives with if only's. What happened,
happened. What you did, you did. You did some things
well. Other things you screwed up. That is now in the
past. Today is today. I give you permission to make a
fresh start, a chance to make new mistakes rather than
relive the old ones. I also offer you a chance to do things
that will make you feel better. That is today. Yesterday is
gone. You can relive it and relive it, but you lose this day
and that is all you really have. It's hard to change that
which has already happened. You can only change it if it
is repeated today and you behave differently.

When you accept the fact that your husband is suffering from an illness today and that chances are pretty good
that he will still be sick tomorrow, you are in a better
position not only to help yourself, but to help him. Pick
a time when you are not angry, and he is not drinking,
and share with him some of your concerns. He may or

may not listen, but the seed will have been planted. Literature about alcoholism or AA left around the house may get an angry response, but is seldom left unread. You are not preaching, but looking at reality. There is a difference. He'll probably continue to deny even after you've stopped, but you will no longer be part of his denial system. And a suggestion will have been made as to where the help is—when he's ready to ask for it.

Embarrassment, Avoiding Drinking Occasions

You cannot take responsibility for anyone's behavior but your own. You are a person in your own right. You are not merely a reflection of your husband. He is a person in his own right. When you go to a party he'll do what he does and you'll do what you do. Concentrate on having a good time for yourself. *Stop watching him. Stop trying to control the amount he drinks.* That is not your problem. He is an adult, and as an adult, he must make that decision for himself. The only decision you have to make, as far as he's concerned, is who drives home. You may have to assert yourself here, but the rest is up to him and not to you.

If you find that having a good time with him is too much for you to handle, go without him. Yes, you may have to start going places alone. As his disease progresses, he will become more and more antisocial and you will find yourself home and isolated until you learn to go out by yourself.

I gave a large party about six months ago. As one of my guests was leaving, she thanked me and apologized for her husband's absence. I hid my embarrassment because, until that moment, I had not realized he was missing.

It will be hard, at first, to go places without him. It will get easier. Go with a friend if you are too uncomfortable to go alone, but go. You don't have to withdraw from outside contact because of your husband. If he doesn't want to go to the family wedding, to your sister's on Sunday, or whatever, take the kids (if they're invited) and go. You'll be amazed, but no one will ask for any great big explanation. They'll be happy to see you. They'll express appropriate regrets that your husband couldn't make it, and that'll be the end of it. Believe me, he's the central figure in your life but nobody else's. Why deprive yourself of having a good time? Why be punished because he is sick? It's unfortunate that your husband is ill, but alcoholism is *not* contagious.

I understand that the things I am suggesting to you are a little scary. You've been very dependent, and I'm telling you to go places alone. It's like jumping into a pool. At first the water feels cold, but it warms up once you start to splash around. The idea of going off the diving board is threatening, but once done, you feel a sense of accomplishment. And, of course, the more you work at it, the easier it becomes.

Shift in Relationship, Domination, Takeover, Self-Absorptive Activities

Even Superman didn't want to be Superman all of the time. He only wanted to be Superman when it served his purpose. The rest of the time, he was content to be a regular person. The same goes for you. You don't have to do everything all the time. Just because your husband abdicates a responsibility, does not mean you have to pick it up. If he has promised to paint the kitchen and isn't doing it, you don't have to do it unless you cannot live with it the way it is.

If he loses his job, it doesn't automatically mean that you *have* to go to work. Taking over the role of the breadwinner is not necessarily the most desirable alternative. Before you panic, find out the circumstances of his losing his job. The fault may or may not lie with him. The reason may not be alcoholism.

There are a number of questions. Is there severance pay? Is he eligible for unemployment? Will the company rehire him, if he enters a rehabilitation program? More and more companies are becoming aware of the savings involved if they do this.

Do you have savings? Are you eligible for public assistance? Will your family help out for a while? Attend an Al-Anon meeting. Ask the women you meet how they handled this particular problem. Job loss is no stranger to those who live with alcoholism.

What I am suggesting is that rather than pick up the gauntlet that he has dropped, you may make better use of this time to take a good hard look at yourself and your situation, and think about what you want to do with your life.

There is the possibility, depending on how sick he is, that he may find another job. It may shock him into facing himself. Your act of heroism may be perceived by him as castrating. Examine your motives. Buy a little time.

This may be the point when you decide that you've had it. You may decide that you are no longer willing to live in this situation. You may decide you want to go to work, because it is good for you and for your children. It may be a desirable solution for many reasons. But one of those reasons should not be to take the burden off your husband. Chances are that he will not make things any easier for you at home, and what may have the potential to be a wonderful growth experience for you will end up making you even more resentful. And just when you are feeling terribly, terribly sorry for yourself because of the burden you carry, somebody like me will come along and say, "Martyrs are rarely appreciated during their lifetimes, but women who have careers and also run households are among the most exciting people I've ever known."

How long can you do it all? Do you really want to? What's in it for you? Just who is impressed or who do you want to impress? Do you want to drain yourself physically and emotionally? Where are you in all of this? Or are you?

What did you do for yourself today? What did you do just because it made *you* feel good? Nobody else, just you. You may resist the idea. That's very selfish. Yes, it is. It is selfish, but not in a negative sense. If you do something for yourself that causes harm to another, that may not be a good idea. But most of the things that we do that are selfish are fulfilling of the self. These things not only benefit us, but those around us. If you feel good, you will influence those around you. You know that others react to your irritability; they also react to a feeling of well-being.

Why not make a list of ten things that you like to do? Most of them probably aren't even costly. Promise yourself that you will do at least one of them every day. Doing something for yourself will help make you feel better about yourself.

This list will probably be hard for you to write. Thinking about yourself in other than a pitying way is a new idea. Try it. There's nothing to lose but a few minutes of misery.

These are the first steps in building a life for yourself in which your husband may or may not be a part. You start with the simple little things that give you pleasure. Then, when doing for yourself becomes a part of your daily routine, when seeing others is a part of your entitlement, you may then start to think in terms of what more productive things you can do with your time. You may want to think in terms of volunteer work, taking a course, or looking for a job that you will enjoy.

The change in focus is what is so important. Do what you do—whatever it is, because *you* want to do it— because it is good for *you*—not because you are afraid to ask him for money or because you think you should. Do what feels right for you. All other things will fall into place.

Guilt

Give it up. It is a worthless emotion. You didn't cause his disease. You can't cure it, nor can you control it.

Let your conscience be your guide. That comes from the inside. That gives you the true measure of what is right for you and what is wrong for you. Guilt is imposed by the outside. Who has the right to decide for you how you should or should not feel, or how you should or should not act? After all you are an adult.

At about this point you must be thinking, "That all sounds well and good, but it's easier said than done!" You're right. There's nothing easy about becoming your own person. It's hard work.

Essentially what I'm telling you to do is to take your power back. You have *given* him the power to make you feel guilty. He cannot do it to you unless *you allow it*. But, but, but. . . . Think about it. The next time he pushes that guilt button say to yourself, "Do I want to feel guilty about that? I'm sorry he feels that way, but that is only my problem if I choose to make it so." See what happens. The pain may be a little less.

Obsession, Continual Worry

Obsession is really rough to combat. It is such a relief if you find that you are thinking of something other than your alcoholic and your problems, if only for a moment. These consume you. They overpower you.

As you begin to think of yourself a little more, the obsession will begin to lose its hold on you. You can, essentially, only think about one thing at a time. If you are thinking about something else, you cannot be thinking about your problems. Concentration under stress is extremely difficult, so do not be too demanding on yourself. Try to concentrate on something else, if only for five

minutes at a time. If that is too long, try it for two minutes or even one minute. The time will build up. Just
stay with it.

Many women have told me that they use the Serenity
Prayer to help slow down and relax. They just repeat it
over and over. It contains a wonderful message.

> God grant me the serenity to accept the things
>   I cannot change
> The courage to change the things I can
> And the wisdom to know the difference.

Try it. Or pick up a book on relaxation responses, or
attend a yoga class, or a lecture on meditation. When
was the last time you enjoyed the quiet solitude of a
church? What about a hot bath? Ride a bicycle around
the block. Find something that will help slow down
those spinning wheels in your head and divert your
mind. It will only work for short periods of time in the
beginning, but the time will grow. Gradually, you will be
in control of your own mind. After all it belongs to you.

The worry doesn't do you much good either. I've never
heard anyone say, "Boy, am I glad I worried about that.
It really helped." I have heard the reverse. "Why did I
waste all that time worrying? It didn't change anything."

That's very true, but it's not going to make you stop

worrying. Instead of spending your whole day worrying about what kind of shape he's going to be in when he gets home, tell yourself you'll start worrying at five. It takes a lot of energy to decide not to worry at all when you've conditioned yourself to worry. It may take a little less to put it off. "I'm not going to worry about that problem just yet." The problem at the moment is, "What shall I make for dinner?"

Another thing to keep in mind when you start to worry is the simple question, "Whose problem is it?" It is very important to know where somebody else ends and you begin. Whether or not your husband gets home safe is not *your* problem. You have no control over that. If you've decided he should be home at six for dinner, that's *your* problem. If you believe his promises, that's your problem. If you cover up for him, that's *your* problem. If he doesn't show up for dinner, that's *his* problem. You're not a short-order cook. If he's hungover after an all-night drunk, that's *his* problem. It belongs to him. Let him have it. You've got enough that belongs to you. You don't have to take any more on. When you start to worry, don't forget to ask, "Whose problem is it?"

Fear

Fear is your constant companion. Some of your fears are rational, some irrational. Some of the things you are afraid of are real. Some are imagined. Some of your fears you can identify. Some are nameless. Some of your fears are healthy and necessary; others are destructive to you.

The first thing you have to do is try and sort out the fears that are working for you, and those that are working against you.

Do you have a friend you can trust? Is there someone who will listen to you, without giving advice, and let you hear yourself out? Just talking about what's going on in your head will help to take the edge off.

You may resist the idea because you don't want to burden your friends. Is that fair to them? When a friend confides her problems to you, how does it make you feel? I venture to say it makes you feel good. Why deny your friends the right to be your friend? Kathy told me of her resistance to burdening her friends. One night her husband laid such a trip on her that she went hysterical and unloaded to her friend Ken. When she finished she felt greatly relieved, but was concerned as to his reaction. "How did it make you feel that I did that?" she said. "Did you feel I was leaning on you? Just what did you feel?" His response was simply, "You made me feel important."

Why deny someone else the chance to feel important when it will also be helpful to you? Just choose your friend wisely. Maybe one of the women you met at that Al-Anon meeting I suggested. Such a person would both respect your privacy and understand your problem. Secondly take a look at your fears and differentiate between the immediate ones and the projected ones. You can, with active alcoholism, live only in the day. You cannot concern yourself with tomorrow. You must focus on getting through each day one at a time. If, for reasons you don't fully understand, you are more afraid of living without your husband than with him, accept that as real for now. Don't deny your feelings or judge their appropriateness. Accept that you are afraid. To deny the feeling is to waste energy. You have no energy to waste and you cannot will the fear away. It will return. Admit to yourself, "Yes, I am afraid. Now what am I going to do about it?"

Violence

You may fear for your life. Many women who suffer from physical abuse are the victims of alcoholic behavior. Although not all alcoholics are violent and not all violent people are alcoholic, more often than not, abused wives will say that he "had a couple."

If you live with violence, or the threat of violence, it is very important to do your homework.

The first thing to do, if he is physically abusive to you, is to stop making excuses for him. You did *not* deserve it. You may have provoked it, but you did not *deserve* it. The fact that he is sorry and promises never to do it again does not make it all right, that is, if he even remembers what he did. You are a person. This behavior is unacceptable. The "If I hadn't said, he wouldn't have" doesn't cut it. Either he would have or he wouldn't have, but the responsibility for the violence is his. His violence is his fault. What you can do is look at what you do to trigger it.

Arguing with him when he is drunk is asking for trouble. There is no reasoning. Remember, you are arguing with a chemical. Berating him will make him angry. These factors will set you up to get hurt, if he is prone to violence. He will find enough reason on his own without your adding fuel to the fire.

He will not like the fact that you are working on becoming a whole person. Manipulative people are very threatened by changes in those around them. He'll try and suck you back in. Standing your ground may momentarily cause more trouble, but as you grow, you will be ready to meet each stage.

Alcoholics are very sensitive to tone. If you say, "I'm going to bed," and what you are thinking is, "I'm going to bed, you son of a bitch," he'll react as if you said what you really meant. Don't play games with yourself. "All I said was . . ." You can fool a lot of people that way and maybe even yourself, but you cannot fool your alcoholic. He is very tuned in.

There are a couple of ways to work on this. The first is to come to realize that you are really angry at the disease, and that your husband is a very sick person. Once you can accept this, the vibrations that you send out will not say "Die" and he will not feed on them. Many women have told me that when they were finally able to accept, on an emotional level, the fact that alcoholism is a disease, the violence stopped. This may or may not be true in your case, but it is certainly worth a try. And second, read everything you can about the illness, attend Al-Anon meetings, and talk about it with other people who understand and have been through it. They will be sympathetic, but will not offer you sympathy. They will let you talk it out and share your experience with you. It will help to take the edge off the fear and keep you from misdirecting your anger.

At the same time, keep in mind that there are other things you can do.

1. You can call the police. They will not take action unless you are willing to press charges, but they can quiet things down for the night. Be honest with yourself when you consider this suggestion. Can you do that or are you more fearful of his reputation, or his losing his job, or what the neighbors will think, than of your own protection? You may be. Many women

find it helpful to call; others find they are unable to.

You may be willing to make the call but he may not let you near the phone, or you know that he will tear it out of the wall if you go after it. This is also a very real possibility. You can ask someone that you know and trust to call you, and if things are not under control, that person can call the police.

2. Never place yourself where you cannot get out. Do not allow yourself to be trapped. Have a door between you and him and be ready to get out if you have to.

Think about what you will do when you leave the house. Be prepared when, and if, the time comes. Is there a friend you can drop in on any time of the night? Is there a women's shelter in your area? Find out. Is there a wife-abuse hot line? Call your local mental health center or local chapter of NOW, and find out. Your problem will not be unique to them. Ask for suggestions. Is there an underground of places for you to go? Stash enough money, and have it readily available, so that you can spend the night in a motel if you have to. But plan ahead so that you don't find yourself on the street with no place to go but back in.

What about the children? Will he go after the children if you leave? Many women stay and face it in order to protect their children. There are alternatives. One is to take the children with you. Chances are they are not asleep. If you cannot take them with you, call the police from the nearest phone and tell them what is happening, so they can help you get them out. If the children are old enough, talk to them before the fact so that you will have a plan should there be violence. The intent is not to alarm them, but for all of you to be prepared. The discussion will be both upsetting and reassuring at the same time. It's a very unpleasant thing to contemplate, but so is the situation.

3. Find out your legal rights. They vary from state to state. Call an attorney or your local legal aid society. You will need to know what legal steps you can take to protect yourself from physical abuse. Your position may not be as bleak as you think. Knowing what it is will help you to realistically assess the situation. You are best off talking to a lawyer who understands alcoholism and alcoholics. The National Council on Alcoholism may be able to recommend someone to you. If not, they may be able to refer you to someone who can. Or ask someone who belongs to either AA or Al-Anon for a referral. This does not obligate you. You may not be ready to call. But have the number handy so that when you are ready, you don't have a delay.

Bear in mind that the decision to live with violence is yours. If you do not feel strong enough to explore alternatives, all the more reason to continue to work on yourself in order to reach the point where you can make a choice. At this point, you may be more afraid to be on your own than to stay. He has helped you to feel this way. All your self-doubts have been reinforced. You believe him when he promises that it won't happen again. You want to—so you do. You feel so isolated. You are embarrassed to discuss what happened and you are embarrassed to be seen. You don't want to have to answer any questions. If, after looking at the suggestions offered on these pages, you still feel as intimidated and out of hope as you did before, I would encourage you to talk to someone who is familiar with this particular problem and how to deal with it. Call that wife-abuse hot line and find out where and how to get help. You don't have to identify yourself. This is not a simple problem and the answers are not simple. You deserve better treatment and you need to believe that you do. You also need to find out how to make that happen. If you knew how to do it yourself, you would have. Help is available. Take advantage of it.

Another fear that you may have has to do with

his getting himself killed, or his killing someone else. This is a contingency over which you have no control. It is also not unrealistic to consider. It is definitely in the realm of possibility. Ask yourself questions like, *How far will his life insurance carry me? Am I prepared to go out and get a job if I have to?*

If you have no skills, you might want to consider getting some. Not only would it make you less fearful, it will put your mind on something else and get you out of the house.

Volunteer work may fit the bill, if you don't have the courage yet to seek employment. It is a step. It is a step toward becoming a person in your own right. You need to feel that you can take care of yourself. You can never depend on being able to depend on your husband.

Susan totaled her car and landed in the hospital. The doctors examined her, stitched her up, and then told her to call her husband to bring her home. She knew that she could call, but that he would be drunk and unsympathetic. As it happened, he was angry that she was late and he had not yet had his dinner. She then called a cab to take her home. She was fully prepared to do that from the beginning. She was no longer denying the reality of her life and could automatically, even under these circumstances, take care of herself.

You will learn to count on yourself. You will learn who you can depend on and who you can't. You will learn to have few expectations from others. If you have few expectations, you are less vulnerable. You won't hurt as much. The less easily hurt you are, the less fearful you will become.

You will learn to control your own life forces. You will not give your husband the power to control how you feel. You will have choices.

Anger

Anger is a very powerful emotion. It can be turned inward and can eat your guts out, or it can be turned outward and you can risk his wiping the floor up with you. It is a gruesome choice. There are alternatives.

If you truly accept your husband as sick, you will be less angry at him. You will still be angry at your situation, but not at him. To deny these real feelings is to con yourself. They won't go away. Anger is a form of energy. We know from physics that energy once created cannot be destroyed. It can, however, change form.

So what do you do with this energy? You get rid of it. You get rid of it in productive ways. You may choose to ride your bike. The exercise will do you good. Scrub your kitchen floor. You will be happy to have it done. I know one woman who painted the whole inside of her house in a rage. When the job was done, the anger had dissipated and the house looked terrific.

If you're unable to sleep because he's kept you up late, and you're too agitated to relax now that he's passed out, why not do the wash? The sheets don't know if they've been folded at three in the morning or three in the afternoon. Nancy once said, "Remember, you don't get the time back. So use it. You'll be too tired tomorrow to do the things you planned. So do them now and rest tomorrow." Makes a lot of sense. You're not living in a normal situation, so it becomes important to be flexible.

Wives of alcoholics have to be flexible. Planning ahead is nice, but don't count on it coming off if your husband has been involved in your plans. You can be sure of following through, only if you are only depending on yourself. He may have offered to help with the grocery shopping. If you think of it as more than an expression of positive intent, you risk disappointment with its subsequent feeling of hurt. If you take it as a personal rejection, or anger at the unreliable son of a bitch, you turn your feelings outward. Have you considered that the person you've most reason to be angry at is yourself? After all, you've set yourself up.

You know better. Every time you're angry because you've expected your drunk to act sober, you're really angry at yourself.

Don't judge yourself. Making mistakes is part of being human. Just try not to repeat the same ones.

Remember the trusted friend. Talking to her may help take the edge off your anger. If your friend too lives with an alcoholic, she'll know what you're feeling. You won't be alone with it. Of course, you may have to offer her equal time to tell you what's upsetting her, but that's what friendship is all about.

Another way to deal with your anger is to get in touch with it while it is still manageable. When something first comes up and you react negatively, it is a different feeling than if you stew with it all day. This is true for any interaction with another person. It can also be true that what you heard is not what was intended. Even in more typical relationships, different people look at things differently. That is made much worse in a relationship where perceptions are distorted chemically.

Sometimes you can just let things go. Other times you can't, and it becomes important to check things out. Check before you are enraged, and pick a time that he is not drunk. You may not get a response that is satisfying, but expressing your feeling will be helpful. Bear in mind, an expectation as to your husband's reaction can lead to disappointment, but the need to express your feelings will be good for you. "It upset me when you said . . ." Phrase it in terms of "I feel," not in terms of "you did." Remember, you are expressing your feelings, not blaming. If you keep this in mind, and this is truly your intent, you will feel better for having said it. I know it's a scary thing for you to do, but the sky will not open and lightning will not strike you down. All that will happen, no matter how your statement is received, is that you will have made another step toward asserting yourself as a person with rights and feelings.

It may also help you to understand your spouse a little better. His thinking may be "off the wall," but he may not be deliberately out to get you. You are so used to being put down by him that you react to everything the same way. It is not unusual for an insecure person to put others down as a way of feeling better about himself. He may even be projecting the negative feelings he has about himself onto you. And there's even an outside chance that sometimes when he criticizes you, he may be right.

It is important to take a realistic look at yourself. It gets too convenient to blame everything on the alcoholic and decide that you are a perfect person. As long as he is acting outrageously and irresponsibly, you don't have to look at your own behavior. Certainly, in comparison, you come off smelling like a rose. But are you kidding yourself? Sometimes aren't you even setting him up so that you will look like the long-suffering wife married to the inconsiderate bastard?

Carol told me the other day about spending more than an hour and a half preparing her husband's favorite meal. It was ready at the time that Ken said he would be home, with a little leeway built in. That way they could relax and have a pleasant chat first. Do you see Carol sprouting wings at this point? You know the rest of the story. He came home late and drunk. She felt very justified in letting him have it. How could he do this to her? After all her work, she was forced to eat alone and his food was all dried up and on and on and on. Carol was looking to me for sympathy and understanding. That I will always give her, but here she was looking for sympathy and understanding for her behavior. She wanted me to praise her for holding her ground and letting him know how she felt. That didn't happen. That didn't happen, because Carol's anger is not justified. The only person Carol is justified in being angry at is herself. She set her husband up. She knew that she could not depend on him to come home on time. He's an alcoholic. So to let him have it is unfair. It is as if she wanted an excuse to vent anger at him because he is sick. He can't help being sick. She has a right to be angry at the situation. It's a stinkin' lousy situation. But

face up to what you're really angry at. You are angry at
your situation. You are probably jealous that everybody
else's marriage is truly wonderful. Everybody but you is
married to Paul Newman. You're angry at that. You're
angry because you're jealous. I'll let you in on a little
secret: Alcoholic marriages are not the only problem
marriages. Other people have problems, too. Some of
them just as serious. Don't displace your anger. Don't
place on your husband anger that doesn't belong to him.
You will not end up feeling better about yourself if you
do that. Examine your motives. Your thinking has
become confused too. You must be able to separate what
is from what you want to be.

Another thing to consider about anger is whether a
particular remark or behavior is really worth your anger.
He has just called you a fucking bitch for the 738th time.
Is there any need to respond to that? Is there any need
to feel upset or angry about that? It is an old tape. It
should be just so much noise. The only thing that is
worth any energy is to ask yourself the question, Is there
any truth to what he is saying? If there is, then you may
look for ways to change your behavior. If there isn't, the
perception belongs to him, and he won't remember he
said it in the morning anyway. The reason I ask the question about all angers being worth the energy has to do
with how you feel when you're angry. Do you really like

yourself when you're angry? If you do, by all means stay with it, but *if there is nothing in it for you, why not let it go?* This does not mean that you condone things that you don't like, but it does mean that you are maturing to the point where you will decide what things are worth going to the wall about.

Sometimes the reason we hang onto anger is because we lose perspective. I started this morning with a stuck car and an hour-and-a-half wait for the tow truck, which was promised within the half hour. I don't have to tell you the feeling. Anger—what a mild word. Rage. And I couldn't let the guy in the tow truck have it because he has all the power, and he probably was not late in an attempt to deliberately aggravate me. I arrived home livid. My cat took one look at me and slinked down the basement stairs. My daughter has more courage and asked me what was wrong. I told her. In her naïveté— after all at the tender age of twelve she doesn't understand that this thing with the tow truck was merely a part of a grand design to get me—she said, "Is there anything you can do to change what happened or to make it right?" Wiseass kid. "No." I continued to go along. "Then why don't you start your day over right now?" What a marvelous thought. Why should the clock decide when my day is gonna start? I'd had a crummy couple of hours, but I could start my day all over again.

And that's just what I did. And the feeling shifted. I lost the feeling of anger that I had, and allowed myself to be filled up with love for a child who, in the infinite wisdom that only children possess, had given me the day. You too can start your day over whenever you choose. You can start it at eight, or five, or whenever you need to get a fresh start. I give it to you, as my Lisa gave it to me.

The truth is that you are in a very difficult situation to deal honestly with your anger. Your husband is sick and it is unkind to be angry with someone who is sick. He cannot be held accountable for his behavior. Yet you are furious. You are really furious at the situation in which you find yourself, but it is nearly impossible to separate the situation from the person. After all, the chemical is self-inflicted. No one is doing it to him, but him. You also know that that is not realistic because compulsion is part of the disease. Nevertheless, if he didn't pick up the drink with his own hand, he would not get drunk, and you would not be living in this god-awful situation. The anger is real. The discharging of it is what is most difficult. Don't deny that it exists. Find ways to channel it that will be good for you. Eventually, a lot of it will leave you and you will start to feel more serene within yourself, and more compassionate toward your alcoholic. That will come with time and understanding and honest appraisal and reappraisal of yourself.

Sex Problems

This is an area of increasing concern to women in alcoholic marriages. I don't know if the concern is new, but the willingness to discuss it openly is new. Women are waking up to the fact that they have sexual needs, desires and rights as well as men. Women are waking up to the fact that they are not possessions, but partners. They are realizing that they don't have to do anything that they do not want to do, and can do anything that they want to do. It's a whole new ball game. I must admit, I love it.

It is important to try to keep your thinking simple in this area, as in all others. The subject of sex gets very complicated, very quickly. In this area, like all others, decide what is good for you and stick with it. If you have a satisfying sex life, enjoy it. If you find his sexual behavior, while drunk, to be degrading to you, there is no reason to submit. Be sure that you do what you do for the right reasons. If you are repelled when he smells of liquor, but are not turned off otherwise—tell him. It would be best to tell him during a time that he is not drinking. It is only fair.

If you are turned off by him, chances are he will try to put the problem off on you, as he has in all other areas. You are probably no more or no less hung up sexually than anybody else. I have had a number of open, frank discussions with groups of women living with active alcoholism. After the questions about physical abuse and repulsion at the odor, the questions are very much the same as in any other group of women. Women are just beginning to accept that it is okay to masturbate, that it may even be helpful in reducing tension. Women are just beginning to accept that intercourse is not the only way for a man and woman to enjoy each other.

These ideas become important in the alcoholic marriage for a number of reasons. Few women in alcoholic marriages take lovers. Their egos have been so badly damaged, and their sense of themselves as sexual beings has been so badly eroded, that they run away from involvement. They also really love their husbands, and would be unable to handle the guilt if they had an affair. So, masturbation or lack of any sexual gratification are the available options.

The reason that it is important for a couple to explore options to intercourse has to do with the fact that so many alcoholics become impotent. The alcohol increases desire, but seems to decrease the ability to perform. A friend of mine reported a comment to me that she had read in a book on sex for the aged. Poorly paraphrased it went, "The fact that you can no longer run does not mean that you have to stop walking."

Here, as with all other things, ask yourself: What do I want? What is good for me? Once you answer, things should fall into place. Your reasons are your own. You may decide to submit because you know that he falls asleep when he is satisfied, and you are rid of him for the night. The romance goes out when the alcohol comes in. Sex, like every other area of communication in the alcoholic marriage, becomes distorted. And you, as in everything else, must focus on yourself and your own needs. Reacting to the alcoholic is no better for you in the sex area than any other. Be true to yourself. This book will help you get to know that self.

As you come to more fully understand the nature of the illness, and as you become more determined to grip reality, many of the other symptoms of near-alcoholism will either disappear or become manageable.

The *protectiveness, pity and over-concern* that you felt will gain perspective. You now know that the protectiveness that you felt was not good for your alcoholic. It enabled his disease and your disease. Pity and over-concern are not helpful either. Compassion and caring are more healthy, and helpful, feelings for you to express. Compassion carries with it understanding, but does not make us weak. Pity weakens the receiver. To feel pity for someone is almost to say that they can do nothing about what they are, so you, who are above them, feel sorry for them. To feel compassion is to appreciate the difficulty that another person faces, but also offers them the opportunity to do something about it. Over-concern suffocates us and makes us want to push others away. In the case of the alcoholic, it gives him another excuse to drink. The concern that one human being has for another is interpreted as caring, and gives the object of the concern options as to what to do about it. We gain strength through love, provided that love is freely given. Both the giver and receiver become richer. No disease has the power to combat the power of love. It is the most powerful weapon in the world. If I love you, no matter what you do, I become a mirror through which you can look at yourself. If I am not rejecting and hostile but continue to love, you cannot use me as an excuse. I do not have to pretend that I accept behaviors that are unacceptable, but I love you as a person. I do not pity you, nor will I protect you from yourself. I care about you, too much to help you to be weak.

By the same token, you will no longer automatically lie for him. It is no longer necessary. Your self-respect is important. You are taking responsibility for yourself and that means, in part, that your husband now has the choice to take responsibility for himself. Your sense of self-respect, coupled with the desire to stop enabling, make covering up undesirable. If you choose to lie, you do it fully aware of what you are doing and what the outcome will be. If you lie now, it is not because you have to. It is because you have chosen to. There is a world of difference.

False hope, disappointment and euphoria no longer have you bouncing off the walls. You have learned that you are the only one who can be responsible for your happiness. You cannot depend on another person to do that for you, nor can another person expect that of you. You are in charge of you and your happiness or unhappiness. You *allow* other people to make you happy or unhappy. It is not automatic. Once you accept this, your husband's inconsistent behavior will have less of an effect on you. He can please you or disappoint you only if you choose to allow him to do so. The power over you belongs to him only if you give it to him. Accept the good and let him hang on to the rest.

Much of the *confusion* is gone. You are now able to make decisions. You are calling the shots. You are no longer trying to understand the thinking of someone who is drunk. If you could, either you would be drunk too, or he would not be. You have stopped asking your husband to think *as if* he were sober. You are now asking yourself to think as if you are sane. I think you probably are.

Lethargy, hopelessness, self-pity, remorse and despair fade into the background. They come up from time to time, as they do in all human beings. Healthy people have ups and downs, too. But you will find that there are fewer extremes and the downs are more manageable. Gail has admitted to me that she really enjoys a good depression every now and again. She really likes to get into it and feel really sorry for herself and withdraw from the world. However, she gives herself a time limit. She says, "I'm going to allow myself to be depressed until three o'clock, and then I will get dressed and pick up the kids and do the other things that I have to do." It works for her. Especially that time of the month that you want to pull your hair out because your body chemistry is askew. Wallow in it, but prepare your exit. Sometimes you're better off having that hot fudge sundae and getting it over with. It can save a worse binge later on.

You've looked at yourself in a variety of ways in terms of your alcoholic husband. We've talked about ways that you can adjust and be healthy. This has mostly been in terms of improving your relationship with your husband. Now let's begin to talk about improving your relationship with yourself.

In order to develop as a whole person, it is important to know yourself. It is important to know what you think and what you feel, what you're like as a person. You haven't had much of a chance to look at yourself. It may be the time to take the time.

I'm going to list some traits that help to make up one's self-image. There are no right or wrong answers. It is a chance to get to know yourself a little better. If you become aware of some things about yourself that you are not especially happy about, you will now have a choice. You can choose to work on that particular aspect. There is no high score or low score. It is an attempt to get you to have a little bit of a picture of yourself.

All our lives we've heard expressions like, "You shouldn't feel that way." What gibberish. You feel however you feel. If you don't like the feeling, you can make efforts to change it, but it is whatever it is. We may not always behave according to the feelings that we have because appropriateness in behavior is more important. I may want to kick that tow truck driver in the teeth, but I may not behave in that way. I will not deny my feeling.

Sometimes we have feelings that are outrageous. Sometimes I feel like chucking my life and taking off for parts unknown. When someone I love dies, my feeling of sorrow is more for myself than that person. I know my children get angry at me when I'm sick. I may not be able to abdicate my responsibilities and take off for Tahiti. I may express my sorrow to the family and say all the right things. I may not consider my children ungrateful if I'm sick because I know that their security is threatened. But I needn't pretend that I feel differently than I do.

If I acknowledge that I want to run to Tahiti, I can sit myself down and ask why. Chances are I've overextended myself, which I am prone to do. Then I can work out a way to slow down. Acknowledging that feeling can help me to resolve it. Judging myself and saying to myself that responsible people do not think irresponsible thoughts doesn't get me anywhere.

If I acknowledge that the sorrow at the death of a friend is mine, I can then reflect back on the beauty of that person and how much richer I am for having known him. I can then share this richness with his family and we can all profit from it. If I had decided feeling sorry for myself was selfish and I shouldn't feel that way, I could not have figured out what I could offer to those who were suffering too, as much as I.

If I did not acknowledge my children's right to be angry at the disruption in their lives when I am sick, it would only cause anger and bitterness on my part when what I really need is rest to regain my strength. If I acknowledge their anger and their right to it, then we can work out ways that the family can pitch in to make things go smoothly for a while. This way they can take pride in their contribution and not feel put upon. They also don't have to feel guilt because of their feelings.

The trait checklist that I'd like you to have a go at can be found in Muriel James and Dorothy Jongeward's book *Born to Win*, published by Addison-Wesley.

Move quickly through the following list of traits. Use a

check mark (✓) beside those that fit your self-image. Use a cross (X) to mark those that do not fit. Use a question mark (?) to indicate the ones that you're unsure about.

___ Like myself
___ Afraid of or hurt by others
___ People can trust me
___ Put up a good front
___ Usually say the right thing
___ Feel bad about myself
___ Discouraged about life
___ Don't like to be around people
___ Have not developed my talents
___ Glad I'm the sex I am
___ Fearful of the future
___ Dependent on others for ideas
___ Waste time
___ Use my talents
___ Think for myself
___ Know my feelings
___ Don't understand myself
___ Feel hemmed in
___ Use time well
___ Can't hold a job
___ Trust myself

____ Usually say the wrong thing

____ Enjoy people

____ Don't enjoy being the sex I am

____ Often do the wrong thing

____ Involved in solving community problems

____ People like to be around me

____ Competent on the job

____ People avoid me

____ Uninterested in community problems

____ Enjoy work

____ Enjoy nature

____ Don't enjoy work

____ Control myself

____ Enjoy myself

____ Trouble controlling myself

____ Don't like myself

Now look at those traits you have marked.

Is there a pattern?

Are they good for you? Bad for you? Both?

Which traits would you like to change?

Think about it. How can you change those traits with which you are uncomfortable? How can you encourage and develop those traits which are satisfying to you? Both are equally important.

If you can't say that you like yourself, does it mean that you don't like yourself? Or does it mean that you haven't cared enough about yourself to even know? What could you do that would make you like yourself better? Maybe start with the basics. Do you get enough sleep? Do you eat properly? Do you tend to your physical appearance? At what times have you liked yourself? What were you doing at those times? Why not repeat it? Are you doing those things that you wrote down on that list earlier in the book? How can you expect anyone else to like you if you don't like yourself?

Take a careful look at those traits and see what they mean to you. Make a little contract with yourself. Decide that you are, for example, going to enjoy nature. Then set aside a little time each day and do it. Another goal might be, I'm not going to worry about wasting time. I'm going to choose to "waste" an hour each day and not feel guilty about it. Or, I'm going to work on the XYZ committee for the local PTA. Little by little, you'll feel like more and more.

You'll gain a real sense of yourself. You'll become a person in your own right, and your position in your marriage will change.

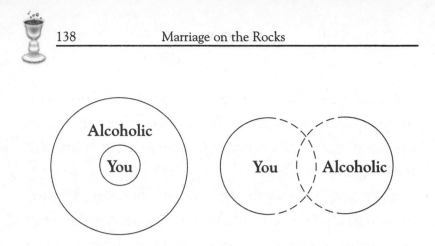

Your position changes from one where you are consumed by the ravages of alcoholism to one where you
stand on your own two feet, and interact with your husband to the degree and in the ways that are good for
you. That interrelationship is flexible, as are all healthy
relationships. Healthy relationships allow for breathing
space. They do not smother.

In order to build a healthy relationship, at least one
partner must be healthy. Only you can decide if your
being healthy is worth the effort. What I have outlined
for you is a lot of hard work. You won't change
overnight, but you didn't get into this state overnight
either. It can't take any more effort than coping with
sickness has taken. But it is a different kind of effort. It
is new. The known is safer no matter how dismal. What
if I get to know myself and find out I really am a terrible
person? There is that risk. There's also the risk that
you'll find out you're someone of value. That is just as
frightening because that carries new responsibilities.

Valuable people take pride in themselves. They don't indulge in self-defeating behaviors. They get their strokes not from the sympathy of others, but from what they are able to offer.

Once you believe you are a person of value, you will be able to offer those things that you need. You will learn that the only way to be sure of receiving love is to give it away. The only way to be sure of being understood is by offering understanding to others. If you care, others will care for you. As ye sow, so shall ye reap. You don't have to react to what is given to you unless you choose to, unless it is good for you. You can act as well as react. You get back what you give. You have that power. I give it to you.

How Your Children Can Be Helped

You will be amazed at the improvement in your children as soon as you start to get better. In my counseling practice, I see many children. As soon as I can, I ask to see the parents, especially the mother. I find that I can be of greater help to the child by working with the mother than directly with the child. Children respond almost immediately to changes in the home climate. When you become more even-tempered and more predictable, so will they. When they see you smile and hear you laugh, so will they. Oh, but where to begin?

Begin with confronting reality. Begin with your children where you began with yourself. Your children have denied as you have denied. If your family is to recover, it must begin with the truth. Use the words that work for you. When you are ready, the words will come. I asked Betsey what she said to her children. They were very young and needed to be told in a way that they could understand. Her children had always asked her questions like, "Why is Daddy doing that?" "Why is Daddy acting so funny?" "Doesn't Daddy love us?" She would answer in such a way as to put them off. They learned that asking these questions would upset their mother and it added to their confusion. Finally, Betsey was ready. She sat them down and very simply said, "I haven't been fair to you. I've been keeping something from you and I'm not going to do that anymore. You know that sometimes Daddy acts like he's somebody we don't know and that upsets you. It upsets me too. Daddy is an alcoholic. He has an allergy to alcohol. When he drinks, he acts in a funny way that he cannot help."

That was the beginning. From that point on, she answered all of their questions frankly and honestly. She offered the older ones literature to help with their understanding of the disease and she made a contract with all of them.

The contract was that they would no longer hide their feelings from one another. If one started to worry that his daddy would come home drunk, he could talk about it. Their father's illness was out in the open. They didn't like it and that was okay. They didn't have to feel guilty about hating their father when he was drunk. They knew now that they didn't hate their father. They hated what the alcohol made their father behave like. A great burden of guilt was lifted.

Children worry. Let them share their worries. The worries will become more manageable. Accept their feelings as valid. "I understand that you're worried your father will have an accident. I worry about it too. But there is nothing we can do about it, so let's see if we can think about something that will make us happy."

Children are fearful. If they can share their fears, you can reassure them. "No harm will come to you as long as I am here. I give you my word," or, "I was afraid to speak up in class when I was your age, too."

The key here is to accept their right to feel whatever they feel. To say, "You shouldn't feel guilty," to a child who believes her father's drinking to be her fault is not going to help her resolve the guilt. It is better to explore the feeling with her.

Ginger's mother had called the police to take her father to a locked ward in a local hospital. The alcohol had affected him to such a degree that he had lost his mind. Life in her home had been unbearable the week before he actually snapped. Ginger felt responsible. She didn't want him around. She wished he would go away. She actually had a dream that he had gone to a hospital. Ginger and her mother had good communication. They had learned to be honest with each other. She said to her mother, "It's all my fault. I made it happen. I wanted him to go away to a hospital. I did it."

She felt responsible for what had happened. She wept with guilt. Because she was able to tell this to her mother, her mother was able to reassure her. She told her that she was not responsible. She told her that she too wanted her father in a hospital. Ginger was not alone in her feelings. She had nothing to feel guilty about. They cried together and it was over. Had they been unable to talk it out, the child would have continued to feel guilty about something over which she had no control.

Find out about the Alateen groups in your area.

Encourage your children to go. Talking to other children with the same problems will be very helpful. It is also a chance to make social contacts with other children who have similar lives. They can be friends without embarrassment. They will learn more about the disease and how to detach from it, but still love their alcoholic parent. If they are not ready when you first mention it, don't be discouraged. They may come around. Bring them Alateen literature anyway. Show them this book. It's so helpful to be able to identify with what you hear or read. The relief I see on the face of a child who says, "Yes, that's exactly the way I feel," is heartwarming.

Understanding their reality is the first step toward turning these children around. They will improve as soon as they no longer feel the weight of the burden as theirs alone. Now it is shared and, eventually, can be discarded.

Confusion has been the norm. This has to be changed. Consistency must prevail. This can happen quite simply. Dinner should be at a specific time. Establish the time and stick to it. Homework is done at a specific time. Establish the time and stick to it. Bedtime is at a specific time. Establish the time and stick to it. You will probably get some resistance at first, but it is usually more a testing to see if the limit is real rather than a rebellion at the limit itself.

Children should have responsibilities in the home. All family members share in the work. Setting the table or taking out the garbage are simple chores, but give a feeling of being needed and belonging.

These behaviors will help to make your children feel more secure. They can now know the parameters of their world and that someone is watching. That someone cares!

This is another key step. There is no way that you can give your children too much love. Tell them how much you love them. Hold them, hug them, kiss them, sit them on your lap. This will not smother them or spoil them. Being overindulgent is not an indication of love. Letting them have unearned privileges to overcompensate for the alcohol is not an indication of love. Buying them things they don't need, because they are emotionally deprived, is not an indication of love. These things satisfy your needs—not the needs of your children. The greatest gift that any parent can give to a child is unconditional love. I love you because you are you. You don't have to earn it and you don't risk losing it. The fact that I love you unconditionally does not mean I approve of everything you do. Sometimes your behavior drives me up the wall. Sometimes it is necessary to punish you. Sometimes your behavior makes me very, very angry. Because I love you, I may not like what you do, but I always love you.

It may be hard for you to be a loving parent right now. When you are feeling irritable and unhappy, it is hard to be warm and understanding. Be honest with your children. "I'm happy to see you, but I'm feeling very nervous right now. Maybe I would be better off alone for a while." Then they know, and if you should lose control, they won't take it as personally. Also, just making the statement will make it easier for you.

Treat your children with respect. If a door is closed, knock before you enter. Their private papers are not for your eyes. They know when you have been in their drawers. They need to be able to trust you. Listen to what they have to say when they disagree with you. You don't have to change your mind, but your listening helps to make them feel they have worth.

Try to be sure that you say what you mean and mean what you say. To say yes or no to a child's request just for the sake of being done with it encourages manipulative behavior. These children have learned from their parents to be very manipulative and it is not a quality to be encouraged. If you do not offer a reason for your decision, that decision may not be accepted by your child. If you change your mind a lot because you didn't think your answer out to begin with, your answer may not be accepted by your child. Either you will be badgered until you give in, or you will become adamant and angry. You need to be able to say, "This is my decision. You may or may not agree with my reasons, but this is the way it has to be. I have heard what you have to say and am sticking to my decision anyway." Then the child has a choice. Either he will do as he is told or he will not. If he does not, then there are consequences for his behavior.

I was at a showing recently of a new film relating to the family aspect of alcoholism. There were many people there. Among them were a thirteen-year-old boy and his parents. I have known this boy for quite some time, and he knows just how to get precisely whatever he wants. He had his mother getting up at 7:30 to fix him a full breakfast that he was capable of making himself—until I came on the scene. I watched him ask his mother for the money to buy a Coke. I heard her refuse. Fifteen minutes later, I saw him with the Coke. I went over to him and said, "I knew you'd get the Coke. I was just interested in seeing how long it would take you." He grinned and walked away. This is a minor example, but it does point up the fact that unless you take control of your home, the other forces in your home will take control of you. As you are getting your personal control back in your marriage, it is also necessary to get the control back with your children. They do not want to be able to get everything their way. They won't admit it necessarily, but children would prefer to be children. If they are not allowed to be children, they cannot enjoy the fight to grow up.

They also need you to say no in situations where they

want to say no and cannot do it for themselves. Sometimes the peer pressure is very great and they cannot get
out of something they do not want to do unless they can
say, "I really want to go, but I asked my mother and she
freaked out!"

Jerry asked his mother for permission to sleep over at
his friend Peter's house on the Fourth of July. His mother
said, "I know the reason you are asking that is so that you
can stay out very late and shoot off firecrackers. That
makes me very nervous and I cannot give you permission." She expected fireworks from her son. He looked at
her and made a remark about how rough it was to live
with a mother who knew the score. He also looked
relieved. He was afraid of getting into trouble with Peter
and his friends, but couldn't let them know he wasn't as
macho as they. His mother gave him the out he required.
She could be the heavy and he could get out of it.

To have said to this child, "Yes, Jerry, I will let you go
because I trust you and I know that you will not do anything you shouldn't," is to invite disaster. That statement is implied, if you have a good relationship with
your children, every time they get out of your sight. But
let's not set them up. Let's not help to put them in posi-
tions that require a strength that insecure, troubled children do not have. To let them know you value them is a
helpful step in getting them to value themselves. That is

the only way you can prevent the things from happening that you are afraid will happen. You cannot stop your children from taking drugs, or acting out sexually, or committing vandalism, or whatever they have decided they have to do. You can help them to value themselves so that these choices are not desirable to them.

I get along very well with the young people I know. My son was curious about this. He couldn't understand why everybody liked his mother, particularly the adolescent boys who didn't like anybody, and whom everybody was turned off to. He decided to check it out. They told him, "We know where she stands. If she says she won't say anything about what we tell her, she won't. If she says if she hears about our brown-bagging it to school once more she'll call the authorities, she will. If she can help she will, but if she thinks we're full of shit, she'll tell us that, too." They know if they reach out their hand to touch me, there will be something there to touch. It will be the same arm that was there the day before, and the same one that will be there tomorrow.

What I have discussed here are all ways to first reduce anxiety and second to build self-esteem. You play a key role in both these aspects. After a while, the children will not only feel better about themselves, they will be able to tune in to you. I was there when Mary Jane said to her mother, "I know that look in your eyes, Mom. You

are starting to worry if Daddy will come home drunk."
Her mother swallowed her up in her arms and said,
"You're right. And if you try not to worry, I'll try not to
worry with you. Let's go bake some cookies."

Many of you are very worried that your children will
inherit alcoholism. We do not really know if they can or
cannot. What we do know is that the home environment
can either encourage or discourage alcohol abuse. It is not
through a discussion of the horrors of alcohol that this happens necessarily, but through the value one places on himself. You can take preventive measures. If there is one trait
that predominates among alcoholics, it is an avoidance of
responsibility. You can teach your children to take responsibility for their behavior. If Johnny breaks the neighbor's
window, it is up to him to call the neighbor, own up, and
find a way to either repair or replace the window. Covering
up for him will not help him grow as a person.

Bob and Tim set a minor leaf fire on mischief night.
No damage was done. The police and fire department
were called. The boys could have lied their way out of it.
But they were wrong and admitted it. They also sat
through a lecture by the police captain about their
behavior. Their mothers went with them. They wanted
the boys to feel the full impact of their behavior, but to
know they were loved. Loved, but not overprotected.
The act of love, in this case, was to let the boys sweat it

out. This way they took responsibility for their behavior.

I have written reports for the court that helped to send an adolescent boy to prison. The following year the parents of the same boy asked me to write another report for the court and this time, I was instrumental in getting the boy off. They know that I will be fair and that the best thing for the child is not necessarily to get off.

If you do your chores, you earn your allowance. If you don't, you don't. Simple, clear. The responsibility belongs to the child. If you make a mess, you clean it up. Or, at the very least, you help.

If you encourage this responsible attitude toward self, not only can the children manage their own difficulties, they can manage their own successes. When they get that A, they get it because they earned it, not because they were nagged into it.

Even the negative stuff can carry a reward. When Johnny told the neighbor he had broken the window, she was flabbergasted. She was so impressed that he had been truthful when there was no way she could find out, that she told him to forget it. He had made a friend.

Encourage your children to talk out their problems so that they can find a way to confront them. Once out in the open, things become more manageable. The solution may be simple—just not thought of.

What I have discussed here are principles that are

important in any relationship with parent and child. They are especially important in the alcoholic home because there has been so much damage to the self-concept. This damage is reversible. If you believe nothing else that I have said in this book, believe that. In fact your children *may be better off for having lived with alcoholism.* What a strange thing for a person to say. I did say it. I have heard individuals at AA meetings stand up and say, "I am a grateful alcoholic." I have heard women get up at Al-Anon meetings and say, "Had I not married an alcoholic, I would be less of a person than I am today." I have heard children at Alateen meetings say, "We are the survivors," and they didn't mean only among children of alcoholics.

These statements are very important and they are not Pollyanna-ish, or naive, or an attempt to make you feel better. They are important because there are very specific reasons why they can be true. First, they are true because accepting the disease of alcoholism has forced these people to concern themselves with their own mental health. Had it not been for this illness, they might not have taken an opportunity for self-growth and self-awareness. They might never have been as aware of proper parenting and how important that really is. We are not trained to be parents and it is a very difficult task under the best of circumstances. Coming to grips with a problem of the magnitude of alcoholism makes one aware of how essential it is that children do not bring themselves up, even if they don't cause us any trouble.

The other part of this has to do with developing scar tissue. We grow stronger because of the difficulties that we have encountered, faced right on, and come to grips with. We do not become stronger if life goes on with relative ease. We don't even know how to appreciate the good things if we have not experienced adversity. These children, your children, as they confront the reality of their lives, will become stronger. The things that bother other children will not get to them. I have seen many children devastated when another child says, "I don't want to play with you." The child of an alcoholic, who is working on himself and his own growth and is detaching from the feelings of rejection by his father, cannot take that kind of remark seriously. "If that kid doesn't want to play with me, I'll find someone else, or I'll play by myself." Those little hurts of growing up diminish in meaning.

If they have joined Alateen, they can talk about these feelings with other kids in the same boat. They can talk about that teacher who is out to get them. The other kids will talk about ways of dealing with the teacher and also, *in a caring climate*, will determine if it's really the teacher who is the problem.

I believe in the wisdom of children. I believe in asking children what they think, especially in the areas that affect their lives. I asked some children I know, who have at least one alcoholic parent, what the best thing their mother could do for them would be or would have been.

These kids are on their way to recovery. They can be up front with their feelings. They still feel the pain, but they are learning to talk it out. That makes it easier for them to hear. I simply made a list of what they said as they said it.

1. Stop the B.S. Tell the kids what's happening. Don't hide anything because that makes it worse.
2. Get the kids into the program (Alateen).
3. Don't put the kids into a state of confusion. Answer the questions they want answered—not the ones you want them to know, the ones *they* want to know.
4. Show the kids a little patience and understanding. They suffer but they don't know why.
5. Don't play God—play Mommy.
6. Don't confront him when he's drunk. It takes two to fight and the alcoholic is always looking for someone to fight with. If he's violent, it'll be your teeth on the ground.
7. Don't make excuses to us. No B.S., please.
8. Don't let the kids know how scared you are. It'll only make them more scared. Try to keep yourself together.

9. Don't have us confront the alcoholic when you don't want to. When my father fell down the stairs she told me to find out if he was all right. He told me to "get the hell out." If she wanted to know, she should have done it herself.

10. Don't use us to get to the alcoholic. Don't say stuff like, "If you won't stop drinking for me, do it for the kids." Leave us out of it.

Children tell it how it is. They are not sophisticated enough to cover up the truth with niceness. Thank heaven for that. We can learn so much from them. They can learn so much from us. We can learn so much from each other. You can learn to love—without strings. You can learn to rejoice in each other's development—without expectations. You can experience the adventure of life together and alone. And if by chance your alcoholic husband should recover, he can join you. Because without him to make you so terribly aware of how precious a healthy family is, you may have missed out on this opportunity.

What "They"
Will Say

Alcoholism is a disease of paradoxes. It defies logic. The opposites of the usual rules apply. What would make sense in a normal situation, simply doesn't in the alcoholic situation. It is all mixed up. When the alcoholic starts to recover and looks back at what he did and why he did it, he can't understand it either. Pete shared with me the following; author unknown, people who identify—thousands.

Positively Negative

We drank for happiness and became unhappy.

We drank for joy and became miserable.

We drank for sociability and became argumentative.

We drank for sophistication and became obnoxious.

We drank for friendship and made enemies.

We drank for sleep and awakened without rest.

We drank for strength and felt weak.

We drank "medicinally" and acquired health problems.

We drank for bravery and became afraid.

We drank for confidence and became doubtful.

We drank to make conversation and slurred our speech.

We drank to feel heavenly and ended up feeling like hell.

We drank to forget and were forever haunted.

We drank for freedom and became slaves.

We drank to erase problems and saw them multiply.

We drank to cope with life and invited death.

You know, because of what you've learned in reading this book, not to say, "If that's what happens, why don't you stop drinking?" You know to leave it alone. You know that the opposite of the usual rules apply. You know that if you care about your husband and want him to stop drinking, you will do nothing to get in the way of his drinking. You also know, because you care about him, that he has to face whatever happens as a result of his drinking. You know that enabling is destructive to both you and your husband.

You know and I know, and the people in Al-Anon know, and the people in AA know, and the National Council on Alcoholism knows and anybody who understands the disease knows. But that is not the general public. To those around you who do not understand alcoholism, your behavior may look strange. You may be thought of as uncaring. "How could she let him spend the night in the drunk tank and not go down and bail him out? What kind of a person does something like that to another person?" A person who loves an alcoholic may do that. But try telling people "I loved him enough not to bail him out!" People will look at you as if you are crazy.

You may receive phone calls from relatives and friends. They will express genuine concern for your husband. They will tell you about the money they've loaned him or the bed they gave him when you threw him out.

They will not be too happy with you. You will then explain to them that your husband is a very sick alcoholic and you are doing the things that you have been told to do if he is to get well. They will say that they understand what you're saying, but if you really cared about him you would. . . . They will not understand, and to some, you will become the problem. "Who wouldn't be driven to drink if he lived with a bitch like that?" What a blow—I never told you that any part of what I'm telling you to do would be easy. It's not.

Your husband will encourage others to put you down. He will turn to them to enable his drinking when you stop. *Enter the enablers.* You're not the only one who has played into this disease.

Friend-Relative

This person, because of guilt or genuine caring, moves in to rescue the alcoholic from his predicament of the moment. He wants to take the pressure off so that his friend will not have to live with this unbearable tension. He pays the overdue bill, or makes the phone call, or provides the bed. He handles whatever it is that the alcoholic does not want to confront. He says he does this because he cares. I suspect it is to serve his own need rather than the need of the alcoholic. What's a friend for? Families must stick together! How could I turn him away and live with myself? And so on. Eventually the alcoholic will run out of these people. They will go just so far and then they will be forced to reject him to protect themselves. Then they will understand you better. "She was right all along."

The Other Woman

Enter the villain of the piece. In your eyes, she is the villain, but there is some predictability to this particular enabler. It may not happen to you. It may. It's not a threat to your marriage. It's a symptom of the disease. After all, you don't want to drink with him anymore. You don't want to go to bed with him anymore. You don't want to save him from himself. You know better. She doesn't. She feels she's the only one who understands him. And she will help him to get sicker. The best thing you can do is to leave it alone. Do nothing to get in the way of it. His guilt will take over or she'll put pressure on for a more permanent relationship. Neither of which is manageable for him.

Jack tried to reduce his guilt by telling Alice all about his affair. He also wanted her to end it for him. Alice knew that this woman was not a reflection on her. She knew enough about alcoholism to know that what he did was not unusual. She knew that she should let him get himself out of it. After all, it was *his* problem. She did just as any normal wife would. First, she let him have it with both barrels right between the eyes in a volume usually reserved for Madison Square Garden. Then she called up the woman and let her know exactly what she thought of her, and what she would do to her if she ever again came near her husband. Right on, Alice! Sometimes you just have to do what you have to do. She felt a lot better. She can go back to being understanding tomorrow. For today, she lost her cool and it felt really good.

Employer and Fellow Workers

Since it takes a long time to develop alcoholism to the degree that it affects your job performance, a man may have been on the same job for ten to fifteen years. During this time he has developed friendships and loyalties. It is only natural for fellow workers to say he came in on time when he was late or pick up the slack in his work. His employer will overlook infractions because he remembers how valuable this man has been to him in the past and wants to believe that he will be again. Without this continued protection and cover-up, the alcoholic could not continue in his job. He would have to give up either his job or his irresponsible drinking. These people are victims of his drinking, but help it to continue. "There but for the grace of God go I." Eventually, the cover-up becomes impossible, but it takes awhile.

The Professionals

It hurts me to have to tell you how few professionals understand alcoholism and, as a result, do more harm than good. Your husband may start to become concerned about how mixed up his life is becoming and, with your urging, he will seek help. The doctor who offers him tranquilizers to get off the booze is helping to get him poly-addicted. The psychologist who tells him that early toilet training and not drinking is his problem is giving him a reason to continue to drink. He starts to believe that when he resolves his emotional problems then he will no longer have the desire to drink. Professionals who understand alcoholism will not indiscriminately prescribe drugs or deny alcoholism as a cause of the other problems. They will refer patients to rehabilitation centers or AA, or attack alcoholism as the problem. Once the alcoholism has been arrested, other problems can be explored. Until then, it is wasted time and money.

It may be small comfort to you, at this point, to know that you have given up carrying the medicinal cask of brandy under your neck and that is the most helpful thing for you to do. The other enablers make it that much harder for you to keep firm in your resolve. You naturally want people to like you. Since you are still feeling vulnerable and insecure, you may start to doubt yourself. It is only human. How much pressure can you take? You will start to get confused. It is essential at this point, unless you are made of steel, to surround yourself with people who understand alcoholism. Talk only to these people about what is happening in your marriage. They are with you. Go to a lot of Al-Anon meetings, or open AA meetings, or call the National Council on Alcoholism for a mental health referral. Do not try to handle it all alone. You will need constant reassurance that you are doing the best thing for you and for your family. You need to be with the people who are on the same wavelength as you are, people who will reassure you that you're not crazy. It may be that, for a time, these people will be your only social contacts. That is not such a terrible thing. After all, they are people like yourself who want to enjoy life. They know they are not strong enough alone to combat alcoholism, but their strength comes from sharing with each other. There is a feeling of warmth and security that will help to carry you over the rough spots. *You are not alone.*

You are not alone, but you are little understood by the general public. Although schools have instituted many fine drug and alcohol education programs, there is little or no emphasis on the struggles of the family. Most of the literature in the field is on alcohol and alcoholism. Gail Milgram, who is at Rutgers' Center of Alcohol Studies, has put together a fine bibliography of alcohol education materials. It includes 873 references. Of these 873, only thirty-eight deal with the effects on the family. Of these thirty-eight, the majority are pamphlets circulated by the Al-Anon family groups. This lack saddens me and makes me angry. It also drives me to write. When you feel stronger and more courageous, why not explore the alcohol and drug education programs in your community? What exposure is your child getting in school? Why not encourage your school system to include the effects on the family as part of their program? The school systems do not leave it out deliberately. They just don't think about it. Maybe it is up to you to plant the seed.

Industry is starting to wise up. Companies are beginning to become aware of the dollars that it is costing them in missed work days and inefficiency. They also know that the investment they have in many of those workers makes it worth making an investment in their recovery, rather than dismissing them. Many large companies are establishing alcohol rehabilitation programs of their own. Employers are learning to offer rehabilitation as an alternative to firing. This is an important step. I don't know of much concern being placed on the worker whose spouse is drinking and who is spending the day worrying about it. This is just as costly to business.

Education of the public is so much of the answer here, as it is in so many things. This is one area where every little bit of knowledge helps. Authorities in the state of New Jersey have decriminalized drunken driving. They are learning that alcoholics are sick people and not criminals. It is a slow process, and an even slower process is that of bringing about public awareness of the profound effects on the family. As you grow more comfortable with yourself, you may feel freer to talk more openly about the awareness that you've gained. Educating the public is the responsibility of each and every one of us. That is, provided that you have reached the point where you are comfortable within yourself on the subject and are not concerned about having others know about your particular situation. It gets tricky because of the social stigmas attached. You may be ready to overcome it, but is the rest of your family ready? Many of the people who speak on alcohol-related subjects from their own personal experience do so using only their first name. Their alcoholic has a right to privacy. You will find that after a while, you will feel compelled to do your part. You will begin to see needless suffering around you. You will begin to be aware of neighbors and friends who have your same problem, but have not come as far as you have. It will become important to you to find a way to offer them help without invading their privacy. You will find a way. You will have to. And you will find the way that works best for you. You will know how to help and what to say, because you have been there—in the same muck as them.

I remember giving a series of lectures on alcoholism and its effects on the family to a group of my counseling students. At the end, they handed in reaction papers. At the bottom of one a student had written, "If I had known ten years ago what I know today, I would not have hated my father until the day he died." I wept for my student, and strengthened my resolve to awaken people to the realities of living with this disease in any way I can.

What About the Future?

That is such a hard question. Who knows? What I do know is that unless you are living in a situation where you are in fear of your life, you are better off not making a decision today. In order to make an intelligent decision that will affect the rest of your life, you need to have your head on straight. It is best, at this point, to use your energies to get yourself healthy. Once you feel in control of your thoughts and feelings, you are in a better position to make a decision.

Many women enter into a game of "If I . . . then he." This is dangerous. What they hope to do is to create a crisis that will cause him to stop drinking. Laudable goal. It just doesn't work.

Mary decided she was leaving Jim. She couldn't live with his drunkenness any longer. Or so she said. What she really felt was that once she left, he would be so miserable that he would beg her to come back and never drink again. She left. She left for a week. She was so miserable during that time that she came running home. She wanted him on any terms. Jim hadn't even missed her. She walked in and he acknowledged her as he always had. Her grandstand play only added to her turmoil.

Another variation on this theme is when you ask him to leave. "If I throw him out, then he will come to his senses. He will appreciate me and the kids, and will stop drinking forever and ever." Talk to Marcia about that one. She threw him out all right. Right into the arms of an enabler. And he's still drinking himself to death. Marcia regrets her action. She was not prepared for the outcome.

I'm not saying never take these kinds of actions. All I'm saying is be sure that if you do it, it is because it is good for you, and not because it will bring him to his senses. You have to be able to deal with whatever the consequences of your behavior may be. It is not usually the loss of a wife that causes the crisis that may lead to sobriety. It is more often the loss of a job. Men identify themselves in terms of occupation. A loss of employment is very emotionally disruptive. This doesn't mean that you should cost him his job. You don't know what will make the difference in your particular situation—if anything.

I've seen so many things that I thought would make the difference and they haven't. I was sure when Joe woke up in a pool of his own blood that he would be frightened enough to get help. He talked about it, but that wasn't his crisis. A year later, when his youngest child looked at him with scorn, he said, "I surrender." There is no way to know. And it is a mistake for you to speculate about what, if anything, will make the difference.

There are a couple of things that you can do. You can be prepared, if the moment ever does arrive, that he comes to you and tells you that he needs help with his drinking problem. Have the 800 number of Alcoholics Anonymous at your fingertips if it is nighttime. Have the local number available if it is during the day. Know about detoxification and rehabilitation centers in your area. Know what your insurance coverage is. Have all these details clear in your head so that when you feel that he is sincere, you can act quickly in order to get him help. That's about all you can do, but it can make the whole difference. If you can move quickly, he will not have an opportunity to reconsider and decide that he can really do it himself. You can't push him into it, but you can make the resources available so that he cannot make excuses. You may go through this more than once, but the major role that you can play in the early stage of his recovery is to have him know that help is available and you want to help him get it.

It may be that you don't believe that this day will ever arrive. There are no guarantees that it will. What if he never gets sober? Do you love him enough to stay with him even if he never gets sober? Can you adjust to alcoholism as a way of life? This is not a loaded question. If you can answer yes, your adjustment will be a lot easier. Rosemarie said that when she answered yes to that question, it changed her whole life. She became much more accepting of her husband and stopped living in a fantasy world. Ironically enough, it wasn't long after this that he became dry. Maybe the fact that she had stopped flailing at windmills made the difference.

If your answer to that question is no, then you need time to plan a life for yourself that will not include your husband. You need to figure out just how you will effect the changes that you need to make. You will need to know what your legal rights are. You will need to know what your financial position will be. You will need to know a number of things. You can talk to other women who have been in your position and who have chosen to leave.

Staying or leaving are individual decisions. All I suggest is that you make the decision on the basis of what is best for you, and not because of the impact it will have on him. If you opt out, do it not out of anger, but because of careful consideration.

Part of your fantasy is that "If he only stops drinking, everything will be terrific." Forget it. Recovery is hard. Life doesn't become wonderful just because he is no longer drinking. It will take him a few months to be able to think about more than just not having a drink. If he joins AA, they will recommend to him that he attend ninety meetings in ninety days. That leaves you feeling neglected. You will have to adjust. He may be irritable. After all, he is facing life now. He has to look at all the things he had been avoiding with alcohol. The bowl of cherries is part of another life. I have no intentions of going into a big thing about the problems involved with sobriety. That would not be helpful. I only mention it to let you know that sobriety is not instant bliss. As it took you and your husband a long time to get sick, you will not get well overnight. Facing oneself is rough. But as difficult as recovery may be, it is certainly preferable to drunkenness.

The future belongs to you. You decide, one day at a time, what you want to do with it. You have a whole full life to live, if you allow yourself to do it, with or without your alcoholic husband. As you recover you will begin to see the ways in which you used your husband's alcoholism as an excuse for your immobility. That will no longer work. You will have to look at yourself. You will take that class because *you* want it, or you won't take it because *you* don't want to—not because he won't like it. You won't stay home because of what he will say if *you* want to go out. You will find out how much you have hidden behind him. If he didn't get in your way, would you have had to face your own fears? What I am saying is this: If you don't join the tennis group because he will have a fit if you're not home when he gets there, you don't have to look at the fact that you're afraid to join the tennis group because you are nervous about your game. You don't have to look at your fear that when they find out how terrible a player you are, they will be sorry they asked you to join. It is a whole other place.

Alcoholism can be a wonderful excuse to avoid looking at things on a deeper level. It becomes a habit. You may not even be aware that you are doing it. Can it be that the part of you that doesn't want to grow up, doesn't want him sober? Can it be that the part of you that wants to be his mother, rather than his wife, doesn't want him sober? What a terrible thought.

What I'm saying to you—in every way I know how— is *get yourself healthy*. If you get healthy you can do anything; the future is yours. If you don't get healthy, it doesn't matter what you do. Stay with him or leave him. You will make the same mistakes. I know many women who have traded off one alcoholic marriage for another. Working on yourself is the answer. Self-discovery is such a delicious life adventure. You will learn your good points and your bad points. Whatever they are, they are you and you can change what you need to, and enhance what you need to, and work to be the best you can be. That's what being healthy is all about. Are you worth it? Only you can answer that!

Getting It All
Together

After reading this far you must have a sense of how David must have felt when he came up against Goliath. You have been coping in a situation of enormous difficulty. As miserable as you feel, you have to give yourself credit for just surviving. You have been going up against the giant with a slingshot. The way that you're feeling today makes it difficult for you to believe how many women have used the principles in this book and are much happier for it. It's a lot of hard work, but it's worth it. I asked a number of these women to offer their thoughts. I knew them all when they were feeling hopeless and alone. I knew them all when their husbands were actively drinking and there was no end in sight. Many of these men are no longer drinking. Some even admit that it was their wives' change of attitude that made sobriety possible. Others continue to drink, but their wives are no longer sick.

I asked husbands and wives the question, "What is the best advice that you can give to someone living with an active problem?"

I include their answers just as they were given to me.

Ruth is a sixty-four-year-old housewife. Her husband is retired and still actively drinking. He does not admit to being an alcoholic.

Keep healthy yourself. I could go on for hours and hours, but that's not the main point. The first thing is for me to realize that I am not responsible for this illness. The treatment for this disease is so different than that of any other. It is contrary to everything I ever learned. If he had the flu, I would make him soup; I would fluff up his pillow and make him feel comfortable. With this disease I have to let him make his own soup and fluff up his own pillow. It is contrary to anything I have ever learned.

Donna is a registered nurse. She has chosen to work only occasionally as she prefers to be home with her four-year-old son. Her husband has been without a drink for about eight months.

I'd tell them to get out to Al-Anon meetings so that they can share their feelings with people who understand what their situation is. People who have lived through it or are in it themselves. That's where I started getting the idea of detachment, not feeling responsible for the alcoholic's problem, and learning that I needed a great deal of help myself—that I finally caught on that I wasn't there for his benefit—that I needed help, too. That's also where I learned to live one day at a time—that I can't do more than that—that's my biggie. When I try to, I really get into a bind. Basically, that's it in a nutshell.

Pat is the mother of five children. She works as a teacher's aide in a class for retarded children. Pat and her husband are both recovering alcoholics.

Detachment is the only word that comes to my mind. Verbal when necessary and physical when necessary. And a complete mental detachment from the disease. Probably, the whole thing should be prefaced with compassion for the diseased alcoholic, followed by detachment. The thing would be to build their own personal strength to the best of their ability. That's all I can think of.

Elaine is an executive in a major company in New Jersey. She and her husband have been happily married for eighteen years. He is recently sober.

Plan to get away—plan to get out—direct all your efforts in that way—financial, job, family. That makes now—today—more tolerable. You are really living for your future, and you have resigned your mind and emotions to that. Also, you don't have to go through with your plan, you can always change it and stay, but you've made all the mental, and emotional, and physical plans to leave. A person with an active problem has to have the ability to survive now, and you can't survive now if you're living someone else's life. By making a mental resignation that you must do something with your life, it takes up the problem of today and living through today and also plans for tomorrow. Time is on your side. You can take all the time you want to plan your future in slow degrees or as fast as you want to, or have to. Be selfish about it. Most people would not leave a terminal cancer

*patient, but that is different because you know when the
end will be. We know with the disease of alcoholism we
could be talking fifteen or twenty years, depending on the
person, and it will never get better without abstinence. So
the decision is what do you want to do with your life. The
other life is out of your hands.*

Donna is a licensed real estate broker. When her husband stopped drinking, she gave up her career and is
now at home. They have a thirteen-year-old son.

*I feel that the most important thing is to learn to
accept alcoholism as a disease. You learn that through
reading and Al-Anon. Something that really shook me
up was when someone said that the alcoholic is addicted
to alcohol, and the spouse is addicted to the alcoholic. I
remember hearing it after I had gone on and on talking
about my alcoholic. I was so embarrassed and angry to
hear that. But once you accept it as a disease and realize how involved you were in their lives—only then can
you start working on yourself and learn how to detach.
I think the best thing is to find yourself and detach from
the alcoholic. I found that for detaching and learning to
live with myself, I had to seek outside help, a counselor,
and then Al-Anon, a combination of the two. I think
those are the important things for me.*

Phyllis is the mother of five children. She works for
the local newspaper.

I think that the biggest problem is the fear. That's the most difficult thing, I think. That's what you have to overcome or work at overcoming. That is the most important thing to do. As long as you show it, the active person will use it to his advantage. As long as they know that they can't create this, then they won't use it. In twenty-five words or less, that's the biggest problem as far as I'm concerned.

Elisa is a first grade teacher. Her husband is still actively drinking.

Stay out of his orbit and stop trying to find a way to get him sober.

Rosemarie is a registered nurse working in a public school. She is the mother of four. Her oldest daughter is about to be married. They have decided not to serve liquor at the wedding. The father of the bride is working hard at staying sober and his needs take priority.

Besides going to Al-Anon, make your own life, which makes detaching much easier to achieve. For me, having a job was the answer. I was able to be me—not the wife of an alcoholic. No one at work knew of my problem. I was able to be free for seven hours a day. That gave me a breather so that I could have the strength to face the rest of the day. Gradually, I was able to learn detachment twenty-four hours a day.

Marty has four boys. She teaches piano at home and has a newly sober husband.

When they call on the phone to say they'll be late, or when they go out "for a while," never ask what time they'll be back. Just say, "Thanks for calling. I'll see you later."

Pauline is a recovering alcoholic. Her husband is still drinking. She suggests to you what helped her get sober.

Learn to detach from the alcohol and not from the alcoholic. Until an alcoholic is left alone to look at himself, he will use you as his excuse to drink.

Bernadette has two teen-age daughters. She is a secondary school teacher. She has determined that her situation is unlivable and is now in the process of divorce.

Al-Anon. Eight hours consecutive sleep, if possible. At least one short rest period per day. At least two peaceful meals a day—alone, if necessary. Necessary steps toward financial independence (quietly). Cash accumulation (quietly).

Pat is a dental assistant and the mother of three children. Her husband has been dry for five years.

I think that one of the biggest mistakes is to think that there is nothing you can do but detach and mind your own business. You have got to be a little level-headed before you can do anything. I got to the point where I decided I was worth more than this, and simply said straighten up or leave. My husband left, got help, and then returned. I was willing to take the risk with whatever he decided.

Gail runs a medical office. She has been married thirty years and has two grown children. Her husband is very active in Alcoholics Anonymous.

Find out about alcoholism. In other words, know what you're dealing with. Get with people who have lived with it and understand it. Share and get feedback. Do something. Getting it out is the hardest step for some people. To decide to look for help is the hardest thing. Keeping it in the closet so long that it must be terrible for some people to bring it out into the open.

Connie is the mother of six children. Her husband is currently in a rehabilitation center for alcoholics.

*Stay out of his problem. Get help yourself **immediately**. That's all that I can think of. Isn't that it?*

Yes, Connie. You're right. That is indeed it. That's it in a nutshell. That's the whole story. It's all been said. Now it is up to you. I could have offered you hundreds of other thoughts, each one saying the same thing in different words. The ideas presented in this book are really very simple. Learn everything you can about the disease of alcoholism. Devote your energy to becoming emotionally healthy yourself, and don't enable the disease. You have nothing to lose, but a lot of pain. You have nothing to gain, but peace of mind. Today is a beautiful day. Allow yourself to experience the joy of being alive. Live in and for the day, each and every day, starting right now.

INDEX